CANNIBALISM: THE LAST TABOO

CANNIBALISM:
The Last Taboo

Brian Marriner

ARROW

Published by Arrow Books Limited
20 Vauxhall Bridge Road, London SW1V 2SA

An imprint of Random House UK Ltd

London Melbourne Sydney Auckland
Johannesburg and agencies throughout
the world

First published 1992

1 3 5 7 9 10 8 6 4 2

Photoset by Intype, London
Printed and bound in Great Britain by
Cox & Wyman Ltd, Reading, Berks

ISBN 0 09 914081 0

CONTENTS

INTRODUCTION

Every time a man kisses a maid and tells her: 'I could *eat* you!' he is perhaps referring subconsciously to some deep, atavistic impulse which lies dormant within us all.

In October 1982 a Japanese student with a near genius-level IQ invited his Dutch girlfriend to dinner at his Paris flat. She was unaware that she was to be the main course. Once inside the flat the boyfriend shot her, cut up her body, and cooked and ate her flesh. He took photographs of the dismemberment process and tape-recorded their last moments together. This must be the most extreme form of the desire to totally possess the object of one's affections.

What we call 'cannibalism' is a corruption of the word 'Carib', the name of a West Indian tribe whose flesh-eating habits were noted by the Spanish conquerors of the Caribbean islands. Later, anthropologists who made a scientific study of the habit of eating human flesh among the world's peoples named the custom 'anthropophagy' – from the Greek 'anthropos' (man) and 'phagein' (to eat). They found the eating of human flesh to be a very widespread custom indeed . . . and it exists to this day.

On 14 July 1970, a man called Dean Baker announced to officers of the Californian Highway Patrol who had flagged down his car: 'I have a problem. I'm a cannibal . . . ' From his pockets he fished out a man's severed fingers. Baker had killed a man and eaten his heart raw.

What justification is there for any writer to devote an entire book to such a horrific subject? One good reason is to remind ourselves just how primitive we remain beneath the thin veneer of civilization, and how *alive* these buried impulses lie within us.

We live in strange times, perhaps at the very edge of the end of time itself. One half of the world is starving, while the other half gluts itself on the flesh of all manner of animals.

We fatten animals in pens so that we might slaughter them to eat. Hens are kept in confined metal cages, spending their entire lives in artificial light to produce eggs for us to consume. Forests are cut down so that the wood-pulp might be used to construct the boxes which hold fast-food hamburgers and the like. We are perverting nature, treating animals with extreme cruelty, and destroying our environment in the process. Truly we have beome mad rats, caught in a maze of our own making.

'Mad cow disease', or bovine spongiform encephalopathy (BSE), was caused by forcing vegetarian cows to eat the offal of slaughtered sheep, demonstrating just how out of touch with nature we have become. And among some primitive tribes, scientists have discovered that a form of madness similar to BSE has been caused by the practice of eating the brains of fellow human beings. People eating people does not, in the long run, make good nutritional sense.

Man is by nature a carnivore – or is he? Certainly we have become so in the last millennium, but have we always been meat-eaters? Some ethologists argue that we were designed to be vegetarians, pointing out that no other member of the ape family eats meat. There is physical evidence for man having originally been vegetarian. We have grinding teeth but no incisors capable of killing prey; and the appendix is the vestige of an organ we no longer require but which was useful for the digestion of roots and vegetation.

One explanation postulated for man's brain-power

increasing so suddenly, in evolutionary terms, is that man learned to eat meat. This released him from constantly having to forage for food. Vegetarian animals spend much of their time eating, having to absorb huge quantities of vegetation in order to extract a little nourishment. An elephant, for example, has to spend eighteen hours out of the twenty-four in grazing, simply to obtain the bulk-intake required.

With a high-protein meal of meat, a man could go for hours without the need for further nourishment, and in those extra free hours he planned how to kill his next meal. This theory of man's origins depicts him as a risen killer ape, rather than as a fallen angel.

Whether man is a natural meat-eater leads on to the question of whether there exists within us a natural aversion to eating human flesh. William Arens, an American professor of anthropology, doubts that entire societies were ever cannibalistic in the past, describing such a concept as being a racist myth, and pointing out that personal witnesses of cannibalism are rare. As this book shows, witnesses of cannibalism were very common and extensive in the last century, in the form of missionaries lucky enough to escape the pot.

We cannot argue with the fact that man is now by nature a carnivore. The vast majority of the world's five billion people eat an astonishing variety of meat. We consume practically everything which flies, walks or swims: birds of all varieties, including song-birds; fish, whales, crabs, turtles, seals and eels. We eat beef, mutton, pork, horse-flesh, and in some cases monkey, bear and dogs.

The Japanese are fond of raw fish – sushi – and such delicacies as octopus and squid; while among Koreans the dog is regarded as being an extremely succulent dish. Snakes are eaten, as are worms, grubs and maggots. Even locusts are eaten, smothered in honey.

We have biblical authority to eat everything around us, as we are told that we are 'masters of the fowls of the air and the beasts of the fields' and we may very properly eat them. There is even the passage: 'You shall eat the flesh of your sons, and the flesh of your daughters ye shall eat.' But set against this is the observation made by St Paul in his Letter to the Romans: 'It is a very fine thing to abstain from eating meat . . .'

Is there a natural aversion to eating human flesh? The evidence would seem to indicate not. Cannibalism is as old as man himself. In *African Genesis* Robert Ardrey pointed out that among the earliest remains of man found – in Africa – was a cave full of human skulls with odd-shaped holes in them. Since there were no other bones from human skeletons in the cave, the best assumption is that the heads of slain foes were taken there for the purpose of extracting and eating the brains. Incidentally, since pottery was not invented until about 6000 BC, human skulls formed a convenient basin or drinking vessel.

A vital clue might lie in the Christian religion's attitude to the subject. The Old Testament, as we know, is a record of human vice and bloody sacrifice; but Christianity and the early Church deliberately set out to banish pagan customs by taking over their ritual festival days and imposing Christian ceremonies over them. Perhaps they turned flesh-eating into the symbolic act of the Communion: drinking Christ's blood and eating His body . . .

Ritual sacrifice had always been a covenant to appease the gods, a fact recognized and adapted by the Church. In AD 1215 Pope Innocent III summoned the Fourth Lateran Council and ruled that the wine and host at the Communion really *were* the blood and flesh of Christ. As a result, many Jews were accused of 'torturing the host' and were cruelly punished.

Let us examine the historical evidence. In 1927 the remains of Peking man were discovered in the Chinese village of Choukoutien, some forty miles from Peking. Later archaeological digs revealed bone and skulls of *Pithecanthropus erectus* – credited with being the first

10

human-like creature to walk upright – and anatomist Davidson Black was able to demonstrate that this early man, who lived some half a million years ago – about 500,000 BC – was a cannibal. From some of the skulls the brains had been extracted, and other charred bones gave evidence of cooking – and of a grisly diet. In many caves and rock shelters which Neanderthal man inhabited evidence of cannibalism has been found. Cro-Magnon man is the first to be termed *Homo sapiens* – 'thinking man' – but he too ate the flesh of his fellow men.

Later arrivals on the scene – Mesolithic and Neolithic man – were cannibals, as was early Bronze Age man. In fact, people eating one another has never ceased to be a custom in some parts of the world.

The Greek historian Herodotus (*c* 480–425 BC) travelled widely throughout Asia Minor and the Middle East to write his history of the Persian wars, listening to oral tradition and relying on his own observations. He reported objectively the local customs in whatever part of the world he found himself, and remarked how, when Darius asked his Greek subjects how much he would have to pay them to eat the bodies of their deceased fathers instead of burning them on funeral pyres, no sum of money could tempt them. Yet when he asked some Indians, who customarily ate the bodies of their deceased fathers, how much they would accept to burn the bodies, not for any price would they tolerate what they considered to be a sacrilege.

In other words, as Herodotus remarked, 'custom is king'. Whatever customs one is born into seem natural. Yet today a taboo exists against eating human flesh, and the practice is regarded with revulsion by the civilized world.

Traditionally, armies always ate their defeated foes as both an expression of scorn and for basic dietary needs. The Scythians did this, as did the soldiers of pre-dynastic Egypt and parts of China. The Tartars were notorious for eating their enemies, and as late as the early

11

nineteenth century human-flesh restaurants were common in China.

It is recorded that Shih Hu, who ruled the Huns of northern China between AD 334 and 349, used to have girls from his harem beheaded and cooked and served at banquets for his guests. The uncooked head would be passed around on a platter so that the guests could note for themselves the beauty of their dish. Could this be the reason why we still refer to attractive girls as being 'dishy'?

Strabo, another Greek historian, writing just before the time of Christ, reported that the eating of human flesh was commonplace in Ireland. St Jerome, some four hundred years later, reported that the practice was still common in Scotland.

Famine was always a great spur to cannibalism. In AD 450 famine in Italy led to parents eating their children. A great famine in England and Ireland from AD 695–700 resulted in 'men eating each other', as a contemporary historian reported. Between 845 and 851 it was the turn of Bulgaria and Germany to starve – and eat one another. AD 963 was the beginning of a five-year famine in Scotland, during which time people began to devour one another. In AD 1069 parts of England were so short of food that human flesh was added to the diet; and during a great famine in Egypt in AD 1201 human flesh was sold openly in the markets.

In the twelfth century, legends of a priest-king named Prester John, supposed to have a realm in the Indies and to have defeated the Muslims, began to go around Europe. Popes, kings and bishops sought to enlist his aid in the crusades against the infidels, and expeditions were sent out to find him and make contact.

Then in 1165 the text of a letter from Prester John to Emanuel I of Rome and the King of France was widely circulated and believed. In the course of that letter Prester John promised to help capture Jerusalem. It was a very welcome message and an extremely popular one, with versions of the letter appearing in many languages, including Italian, German, English, Russian and Hebrew.

In it Prester John also wrote: 'We have in our country still another kind of men who feed only on raw flesh of men and women and do not hesitate to die. And when one of them passes away, be it their mother or father, they gobble him up without cooking him. They hold that it is good and natural to eat human flesh and they do it for the redemption of their sins.'

Marco Polo, at the end of the thirteenth century, set out on a twenty-four year journey from Venice which took him to the Far East and China. His story of his travels, as dictated to another man while in prison, was a best-seller for the time; and in the course of that book Marco Polo recounted how many Chinese and Tibetan tribes ate human flesh.

Amerigo Vespucci – after whom America was named – voyaged there a decade after Columbus, and wrote about it: 'There are people in that place . . . who go about entirely naked . . . and who feed eagerly on the flesh of their conquered foes.'

The Turks long had a reputation for sheer savagery, and in 1564, when they defeated the Polish leader Wisniowiecki, they tore out his heart and ate it. And it was quite common for Chinese executioners to eat the hearts or brains of their victims.

Most of our information about the flesh-eating habits of various tribes came from travellers, the most persistent of whom were missionaries. It was they, the butt of countless jokes about missionaries in cooking-pots, who sent back detailed accounts of cannibalism in 'Darkest Africa'. Their letters, in the nineteenth and early twentieth centuries, to their various headquarters in London and elsewhere, formed a mass of detailed eyewitness accounts by people whose veracity could not be doubted.

And it appears from these reports that for the vast majority of the world, with the exception of Europe, the eating of human flesh was considered to be a quite normal human acitivity.

When one considers cannibalism, it is important to bear in mind that there was no instinctive aversion to eating human flesh, and primitive people probably made no distinction between the flesh of animals and men. Our modern aversion is the product of our civilization. Or should that be aversions? Most of us might feel revulsion at the thought of eating a dog – but not the Koreans. The pig is abhorrent to Semitic peoples, while we English enjoy our bacon.

One form of cannibalism, practised extensively throughout Europe for several centuries, has been the custom of utilizing human remains in medicines. Lemery's Medical Dictionary, a standard medical text in the eighteenth century, listed almost every part of the human body as having medicinal qualities, and the still warm blood of hanged felons was often given to epileptics and other patients waiting by the scaffold. Today, heart and lung, kidney and other organ transplants are common. Yet what is this if not cannibalization of the human body? It is all a matter of custom . . .

Some scientists believe that the practice of eating human flesh was a cult dictated by some religious ideology. This is too simplistic a view. The early history of cannibalism was indeed one of human sacrifice to propitiate the gods, but there were other factors. Primitive tribes believed that to eat the flesh of slain foes would imbue them with the natural forces and virtues of the enemy. Sometimes it was done for revenge. Sometimes there was even a sexual motive.

In short, cannibalism was either connected with religious rites and ceremonies – witness the human sacrifices of the Incas and Mayas – or there was a plain dietary need for protein-rich food.

In Africa and Australia, it was felt that to eat dead relatives was to honour them. It was also, of course, a cheap form of funeral. It was also practised as a form of population control. In the nineteenth century there was one tribe of Aborigines which ate every tenth baby born.

In the Congo, slaves were deliberately fattened for sale as food in the markets. Fijian chiefs had to eat human flesh by custom whenever they had their hair cut. In Nigeria, bodies were cut up and devoured in ritual ceremonies.

In Australia, the bush-men dried the bodies of the dead by smoking them over fires, thus preserving the flesh into something resembling beef jerky. Some African tribes preferred to allow corpses to rot before dining on them, while others burned the bodies and mixed the resulting ashes with liquid to make a drink. An early form of our instant reconstituted meals . . .

A South American tribe had children by captive women simply to ensure a regular supply of human flesh. Early anthropologists wrote about the desire for human flesh as a lust and craving similar to what which we now attribute to heroin addicts. There is no doubt that much of this reporting was sheer sensationalism. If some tribes preferred human flesh to the local animals, it was no doubt because 'long pig', as some tribes termed baked human beings, was guaranteed to be more tender.

The revenge motive was sometimes plain. The conscious victim would have a limb removed and have to watch it being cooked and then eaten before his eyes. He might even be offered a portion as a gesture of supreme contempt.

Among some tribes there persisted the superstition that by eating the body of a dead man, it would prevent his ghost from returning to haunt the tribe. One tribe punished adultery by eating the woman in question.

The transference-of-powers belief lay behind some flesh-eating: the belief that one could possess the qualities – the courage, speed and skill – of a foe by eating him. Another example of 'sympathetic magic', among some tribes a man with a bad leg, for example, would eat the good leg of a corpse in the belief that it would transform

15

his own limb back to health. Aborigines believed that for a child to eat his deceased father would endow the child with the father's hunting skills. The Maoris ate the eyes of men they slew in battle. Some tribes simply drank the victim's blood; others required the flesh too.

However, modern research with the simple planerium worm has discovered an astonishing fact. This simple organism can be trained to work its way through a maze to find food. It involves a long process of trial and error. Yet if that planerium worm is cut and fed to other planerium worms, they 'inherit' the ability to master the maze immediately. Is *this* how man evolved: through eating the brains of his fellows?

It can be seen that the motives behind the eating of human flesh were not as simple as might be supposed. But it is a good bet that among early mankind human flesh was viewed as a valuable source of protein.

The book falls naturally into four main parts:

(1) Those who ate human flesh as a religious ceremony.

(2) Those who ate human flesh because they were *forced* to by circumstances. Sheer necessity – the need to save one's own life – is accepted by Catholic theologians as a justification for cannibalism. For example, the Uruguayan rugby team that crashed in an aeroplane in the Andes in 1972. The sixteen survivors, kept alive for seventy days by eating flesh from the bodies of their dead companions. (See Part II, chapter 5.)

The classic English case was that of the *Mignonette* survivors in 1884. When the ship foundered in a heavy gale, the captain, a seaman and the cabin boy, took to the lifeboat. On the seventeenth day adrift, with no food, the captain and seaman agreed to kill the cabin boy and eat him, which they did. Eventually they were picked up by a passing freighter. Back in England they were tried for murder on the high seas. The jury very nearly returned with a Not Guilty verdict because of the circumstances, but the two men eventually served six months' imprisonment. (See Part II, chapter 4).

It is important to remember that at this period cannibalism at sea was almost routine when sailors were shipwrecked and ran out of food. It was even called 'the custom of the sea', and was regarded as quite legitimate – providing straws were drawn to determine who was to be on the menu. It still goes on, but without any question of a lottery. In 1988 it was reported that South Vietnam refugees, adrift and lost in a leaking boat, began to kill and eat each other when food ran out. Four people, including two children of eleven and fourteen years, were beheaded, dismembered and their cooked flesh distributed among all on the boat.

Something very similar certainly happened to Sir John Franklin's lost expedition to the Arctic in 1845. Although there were no survivors, later eyewitnesses who came upon their remains wrote to the Admiralty stating that cannibalism had undoubtedly occurred, citing as evidence of this: 'the mutilated state of many of the corpses and the contents of the kettles'.

It has been revealed that from sheer necessity, the Russians resorted to eating the bodies of the dead during the siege of Leningrad in 1942; and there are documented cases of inmates of concentration-camps eating human flesh.

(3) Those who eat or procure human flesh for *economic* motives. The grisly German trio of Haarmann, Grossmann and Denke actually sold human flesh for meat after the First World War when food was in short supply, murdering people to procure their flesh, which they passed on to their unsuspecting customers, thereby turning them into unwitting cannibals.

Sawney Beane, who lived in the reign of James I of Scotland, fed his large family on human flesh simply because it was easier to catch and more abundant than venison.

(4) Finally, we come to those who eat human flesh because they *like* it. Usually there is a sexual element present in our modern-day cannibal case. In our cities,

the centres of our high-culture levels, there exist yet the eaters of human flesh – not from necessity, but from a perversion of the most gruesome kind.

The book charts a journey through the dark depths of the human psyche, but we also laugh at what we fear most – hence cartoons about missionaries in cooking-pots. And Dean Swift's *A Modest Proposal* . . . used grim irony to suggest that in order to alleviate the suffering of the starving Irish people, babies might well be boiled and served with spinach.

And what of cannibalism in the future? The world's population is expected to reach six billion by the mid-1990s. Many experts predict that the arms race will be abandoned in favour of a food race. Wars will be fought to preserve the dwindling food supplies of nations unable to feed their teeming millions. At that point human flesh might well once again be viewed as a prime source of protein.

PART I: THE CULT OF FLESH-EATING

1
THE AZTECS

Every now and again a story surfaces in the newspapers about the discovery of a lost 'Stone-Age' tribe living in complete ignorance of the delights of the twentieth century. Usually such tribes are found in the remote interior of New Guinea or along the Amazon. Very quickly, of course, we 'civilize' these people, so that the women begin wearing bras and plastic sandals, while the men sport Bermuda shorts and sunglasses and wonder how on earth they managed without them for thousands of years.

Such was the situation with the Aztec empire. While the rest of the world was busy making ships, guns and printing presses, and generally warring with one another, the Aztecs carried on a primitive yet highly stylized system of their own, completely unaware of the existence of the outside world. More importantly, they still worshipped the sun when others worshipped either Christ or Allah.

The cruel clash of cultures when the Spanish discovered them has been dramatized and recorded in many books. Quite simply, Cortés and his conquistadors enslaved the Aztec people and robbed them of their religion and dignity, inflicting terrible cruelties upon them in the name of Christianity. Before Cortés' invasion, it is estimated that the population of central Mexico stood at some twenty-five million inhabitants. Within twenty years the Spanish had slaughtered twenty million people.

The Aztec culture was like no other on earth, and

seems to have been composed of elements and features borrowed from many other cultures. Although they left few written records of their own, the Spanish conquerors of the Aztec empire did write accounts of what they found. For example, the Letters of Information sent by Hernán Cortés to his emperor Charles V, and also the *True History of the Conquest of New Spain* by Bernal Diaz del Castillo. These were accounts of the rites and ceremonies of the Aztecs, with descriptions of their temples. There were also further written accounts by early Roman Catholic missionaries. But since these writers could not speak the language of the Aztecs and had no sympathy for them, the accounts lack any real insight.

What we do know is that the fertile central valley of Mexico was first settled by the Mayas, who were toppled by the Toltecs in the ninth century. The Toltecs declined after the fall of their city, Tollan, in AD 1168, and the rise of the Aztecs began.

According to their own traditional history, the Aztecs were originally a nomadic tribe. In the twelfth century they departed from their traditional home of Aztlan, where they had lived for over a thousand years, and attempted to settle in central Mexico.

They record that they were regarded as being little more than barbarians when they first arrived in the area. It was not until the reign of Itzcoatl (1428–40) that they began to ascend to the leadership of the area, defeating their neighbours and adopting some of their customs, religious rites, and most importantly, their agricultural skills.

Both the Mayas and the Toltecs appear to have practised human sacrifice in their ceremonies, and the Aztecs were to develop this into a high art.

The core element of Aztec religious belief was that in order to ensure that the sun continued its daily passage across the skies, bringing fertility to men and crops, regular human sacrifices had to be made.

Much of this ritual had been common to both the

Mayas and Toltecs; but what the Aztecs did was to adopt and refine the idea of sun-worship by identifying their king with the sun itself. To ensure the health and fertility of their maize god, Uitzilopochtli, a never-ending supply of human hearts was essential. And a vital part of their ceremonies was the ritual eating of human flesh . . .

In addition to the sun god, the Aztecs worshipped many other deities, both male and female, and principal among these lesser gods was Teteoinnan, the earth mother. At the time of the harvest festival ceremony, a female victim was flayed alive and her skin brought to the temple. The priest donned the skin and assumed the identity of the goddess. This wearing of the skin was a typical element in the transfer-of-soul idea, by close contact with the skin and blood of a sacrificial victim.

The Aztec rituals tended to become increasingly more complex and elaborate as time went on, due mainly to their peculiar calendar, which divided the year into eighteen periods of twenty days each. Since each period coincided with the natural seasons of the annual cycle, they had to be marked by special ceremonies.

In February children were sacrificed to the gods of rain and water to prevent a drought later in the year. At another festival – to mark the success of the harvesting of the maize crop – the blood of the children was collected by the priest, who kneaded it with maize dough to form an image of the maize god, Uitzilopochtli. The heart of the resulting image was cut out and presented to the reigning king to eat, while the remainder of the image was cut into portions and distributed among the high-ranking notables.

Totec, the moon god, had to be propitiated immediately before the sowing of the first seed. For this purpose the blood of children would not suffice. The sacrificial victim had to be a prisoner captured in the battles which the Aztecs carried out continuously with neighbouring states to ensure a plentiful supply of sacrificial victims. The more courageous the prisoner had proved himself in battle, the better gift to the god he became. The usual method of sacrificing such a victim was to fasten him to a wooden frame and then fire arrows into his body, so that his outpouring blood symbolically fertilized the soil.

Sometimes, while still alive, the victim was removed from the frame and laid across the stone altar, where the high priest would use an obsidian knife to rip out his heart and hold it aloft, still palpitating, to the sun. The priest would then don the victim's skin, which had been carefully flayed, while his flesh would be distributed to those who had captured him so that they might eat it.

Every aspect of the sacrificial ceremony was full of symbolism and had to be carried out in a precise manner. One blunder by the priest could ruin the entire ceremony. The victim was first stripped of clothing and any ornaments he might be wearing. When he was laid across the temple altar – a huge curved slab of stone – his head, arms and legs would be held rigid by five priests while the high priest ripped open the victim's chest.

After holding up the heart, the priest then placed it in a ceremonial basin which had been carefully placed to collect the blood which poured from the victim's body. Drained of blood and bereft of its heart, the body was of no further use for ritual purposes, and so it was thrown down the giant stone steps of the temple – which were constructed like stepped pyramids – to the waiting crowd below. There it was swiftly cut up and its flesh given to the warriors, and eaten. It was a very religious ceremony, serious and ritualized – far different from the typical cannibal feast.

January saw the climax of the Aztec year, involving several festivals and sacrifices to the god of fire. For three years out of every four the victims sacrificed were animals; only on the fourth year was human flesh required, and then it had to be that of young couples, newly married for the purpose. Once adorned in rich and elaborate robes, they were then thrown as couples into the flames, the charred bodies being raked out of the fire by the high priest's attendants so that their hearts could be retrieved. Other forms of sacrifices during these festivals included drowning, burning, decapitation and burial alive.

Anthropologists have established that similar customs prevailed among other tribes of Central and South America – notably, among the Incas of Peru and tribes in Ecuador – these tribes presumably having been influenced by the Aztecs. The practice of human sacrifice, the dedication of the flesh and blood of young men and women to the gods, reached its apotheosis in the fifteenth century. The end of such customs was invariably brought about by contact with Europeans.

The Aztec king Montezuma was a contemporary of Christopher Columbus – which shows how recent all this was in historical terms – and the Spanish, very properly shocked, soon put an end both to Montezuma and Aztec customs. But primitive superstition is very difficult to eradicate, and 22–23 April remained an important date among many tribes, especially the Pawnee Indians. As recently as 1838 there were reported cases of such sacrifices on this date, bearing a striking similarity to the Aztec ceremonies.

But it can readily be seen that the practice of eating human flesh in this type of ceremony had no dietary significance. There was no lust for human flesh, but rather a pious and highly developed philosophy of pleasing and fertilizing the gods with living human blood, the vital energy of young people.

The Aztecs were Indians who had abandoned their nomadic existence in favour of the city life pioneered by the Mayas. But their tribal, ritual customs were not lost, merely elaborated. And among other Indians, the same grisly ceremonies remained sacrosanct.

To modern eyes such customs seem implacably cruel, but it must be remembered that they took place in primitive societies where the importance of the individual was not recognized. Like all totalitarian states, the society itself came first, and its individual members were disposable in the common good.

2
NORTH AMERICAN INDIANS

In real life, the North American Indian brave was never as noble a creature as he was presented in the stuff of fiction. He lived a very primitive and basic existence and was prey to all the diseases around him. And in his customs he was brother to the Aztecs and Incas.

The most famous tribes lived on the great plains of the American West, and numbered among them the Mohawk, Comanche, Sioux, Pawnee, Blackfoot, Ojibwa, Apache and Cherokee, among others. Such names have become familiar to us through the medium of the motion picture. Although each tribe had its own legends and customs, there were striking similarities – a classic example of Jung's 'collective unconscious'.

One tribe which never featured in fiction were the Kwakiutl Indians, who lived on the remote American-Canadian border. They lived by hunting, as did all other Indians, and because they lived by the Pacific, they were fishermen too. Nomads do not, by nature, like agriculture, which is the first level of civilization.

They were an isolated tribe, living in an inhospitable region with the Rocky Mountains for a backdrop and the north Pacific facing them. On either flank lay the vast forests of British Columbia.

Perhaps because of their isolation, they developed a rich and individual mythology not found among other tribes. They had no concept of time, but the basic tenet of their belief was that at some unimaginable time in the past, the mythical creator and ancestor of the tribe had come out of the sea to found their race. Each member of the tribe was brought up to remember a long list of tribal legends, since they could only be passed on orally, and each was made conscious that the various spirits which protected the tribe could not be depended on to do so permanently. Every spirit had to be rewarded; favours could only be gained with a bribe.

The task of each individual member of the tribe was to seek out his own favourable spirit and reward it so that it might lend him some of its powers. The choice of spirit was very important, and advice was given by the tribal elders as to which spirit would suit a particular individual. But once a Kwakiutl had found his spirit, and was obviously under its influence, then he was deemed to be superior to his fellows.

The medicine men or shamans of the tribe would advise on the choice of spirit. The most fearsome of all the spirits was Baxbakualanuxsiwae. The name translates as: 'He-who-is-the-first-to-eat-man-at-the-mouth-of-the-river'. It doesn't take much imagination to guess that this spirit was a cannibal.

This spirit was reputed to live on the slope of a mountain whose summit was on fire – obviously a reference to a volcano. His household was unusual, to say the least. He lived with his wife, Qominoqa, who procured his daily meals of human flesh. She had the help of a female slave, Kinqualalala, whose job it was to collect corpses to stock the larder. Above the door of the family home was perched another slave, a raven named Quaxqoaxual-anlxsiwae, whose particular function was to eat the eyes from the remains of bodies discarded by his master. His companion was another bird, Hoxhok, with a vicious beak which could split a human skull with one blow to peck out the brains. The final member of the family was a grizzly bear, Haialikilal.

Young Kwakiutl who decided to seek the patronage of Baxbakualanuxsiwae would join an elite group within the tribe, called the Hamatsas, hunters who alone had the privilege of eating human flesh. And that flesh could come from an enemy slain in battle, from a captured foe, or even from a member of his own tribe. The young initiate became, in effect, a licensed cannibal.

But his privileges were bound by certain duties and taboos. He had to perform certain dances and wear special masks. His apprenticeship was a test of endurance. He had to spend at least three months alone, in isolation out in the forest, to prove his devotion to the spirit. He had to learn mysterious shouts and cries. At his initiation dance, he had to fiercely attack fellow members of the tribe and attempt to bite pieces of flesh from their bodies. This would prove that he was indeed possessed by the spirit. Finally, when the elders of the tribe went to seek him out at the end of his self-imposed vigil, he had to have a store of human flesh to show them, saying: 'These are my travelling provisions, which Baxbakualanuxsiwae himself has given to me.'

Actually, the flesh came from dead ancestors. The custom of the Kwakiutl Indians was to place their dead in wooden chests, which were then hauled high into the trees and exposed to the wind and sun. The result was a process of mummification.

When the flesh was required for the initiation ceremony, the elders of the tribe would lower a body and soak it in salt water, before carefully removing the flesh from the bones. This was then placed in front of the initiate's camping site, to be duly 'found' by him.

In the presence of the elders, the initiate had to eat the flesh in four mouthfuls, being careful not to chew but to swallow the flesh whole. Then he was required to drink sufficient salt water to make him vomit up the gobbets of flesh, which were carefully examined to ensure that there were four portions of flesh and no less. If one piece was missing, the initiate's excreta would have to be examined to account for it.

The rules for the new initiate were complex. For the first four months after the ceremony he had to wear a piece of soiled cedar bark. He had to live alone and have no visitors. He had to eat from a bowl and with a spoon which had not been touched by any other members of his clan. At the end of the four months he had to throw his bowl and spoon away in a place where no one would ever find them.

When he drank, the Hamatsa must never take more than four mouthfuls of water. He had to drink through a hollow bone and not allow his lips to touch the water directly. For a period of sixteen days after eating human flesh he was forbidden to eat any warm food, do any work, or have intercourse with any woman.

Part of the legend of the spirit Baxbakualanuxsiwae was that at the moment of seeking flesh, he would cry out in a terrible voice: 'Hap! Hap! Hap!' In his ceremonial dance around the camp fire, the Hamatsa would become possessed with a lust for human flesh, and then begin biting anyone near him, uttering the cry of 'Hap! Hap! Hap!'

The customs of the Kwakiutl Indians became known only when Europeans came into contact with them and questioned them. Sometimes Europeans actually witnessed the flesh-eating ceremonies. But gradually, due to the influence of Europeans, the practice of eating human flesh died out. It became instead a symbolic act, when the initiate would bite just enough to draw blood rather than to actually eat, and the ancient ceremonies became refined into a ritual dance with others who pretended either to be eaters or to be the eaten.

3
AFRICAN APPETITES

Cannibalism was widely practised in Africa – some twelve million square miles straddling the equator and stretching from the Indian Ocean to the Atlantic. If the various tribes displayed one distinctive trait, it was the lack of any religious motive for their choice of diet. They ate human flesh because they *liked* it. That, and because it served as a supreme form of revenge . . .

We owe what knowledge we possess about Africa in the last century to despairing letters sent home by the early missionaries, who laboured long to convert the heathen to a belief in one God. Writing of a Nigerian tribe called the Mambilas, in 1831, C. K. Meek wrote: 'All the Mambilas were cannibal until recently . . . They ate the flesh of their enemies killed in war, and among the enemies might be members of a neighbouring tribe with whom they had intermarried when at peace. Thus it might happen that a man would kill and eat one of his own relatives . . . but it was decreed that if a man killed and ate his father-in-law, he would fall ill and die. There is evidence, too, that these groups sometimes sold their dead for food.' However, women of the Mambila tribe were expressly forbidden to eat human flesh.

Another tribe, the Tangale, were head-hunters who ate only the flesh of men's heads. The Rubakuba tribe were also cannibals, but they made a point of presenting human flesh first to the old men of the tribe, reasoning that they needed young flesh to rejuvenate them. This practice was also the custom among the Zumperi tribe, and, in general, the old were favoured among all tribes.

The Kaleri were the most fearsome cannibals, and would eat anyone, black or white, who dared intrude into their territory. The Yergum kept the bodies of slain enemies for ten days before feasting on them, and then the heads were reserved for those warriors who had actually killed in battle, the rest of the flesh being distributed among the rest of the tribe, women and children included.

The Sura would eat the flesh of any woman of the tribe convicted of adultery, or of any member who had violated tribal law.

Human flesh was rarely eaten raw. Generally it was cooked by all tribes, either by boiling or by roasting. The Jarawa cannibals used to separate the head and cover it in clay, putting it whole in the fire to bake.

The anthropologist P. A. Talbot, writing at the same time as Meek, observed that cannibalism bore no connection with any religious rite or belief, but was practised because of a sheer lust for human flesh. 'Human flesh is preferred above all other flesh for its succulence, and that of the monkey is generally considered to come next. The parts in greatest favour are the palms of the hands, the fingers and toes, and of a woman, the breast.'

Some tribes tortured the prisoners before eating them. The Bafum-Bansaw tribe used boiling palm oil to give their victims an enema, using a special gourd to force it into the victim's bowels. The bodies were then left until the oil had permeated them. It was believed to make the flesh more tender.

The Ibo country was noted for its cannibal feasts. George Basden, a missionary, writing of an Ibo boy who had been placed by his father in the mission to receive instruction, said that the father came to visit the missionary to advise him on his diet. 'He solemnly asserted that it would be of great benefit to his son if he were provided with human flesh sometimes as part of his diet. He maintained that if this were done, a proper man's spirit would develop in the lad.'

Another missionary, Father Bubendorf of Freiburg, whose mission was near Onitsha, reported seeing a group of captives outside the hut of a tribal chief. He wrote: 'Every moment, men, women and children passed me. One would be carrying a human leg on his shoulder, another would be carrying the heart or lungs of some unfortunate Kroo-boy in his hands. Several times I myself was offered my choice of these morsels, dripping with gore.'

Bishop Crowther wrote: 'Cannibalism is widespread from the delta of the Niger for a long way up its course. Among the Okrika tribe, a hundred and fifty prisoners were taken from a tribe on the opposite side of the river and divided among the chiefs . . . They were killed and devoured by them.' He also noted that young boys were kept in pens and fed with bananas to fatten them, before being slaughtered and baked.

The Congo basin was another prime habitat of man-eating tribes. Originally known as the Belgian Congo, this vast area is the dark heart of Africa itself. The Congo River meanders for some three thousand miles before reaching the Atlantic Ocean, and has many tributaries. Along its banks for most of its length lived many different tribes, nearly all of whom practised cannibalism.

Sidney Langford Hinde, in a book published in 1897, wrote of his experiences as a soldier in the Congo Free State Force, and remarked that the captains of the steamers which plied across Lake M'Zumba reported that natives were coming aboard with tusks of ivory 'with the intention of buying a slave, complaining that *meat is now scarce in the neigbourhood*'.

He went on: 'There is not the slightest doubt in my mind that they prefer human flesh to any other. During all the time I lived among cannibal races I never came across a single case of them eating any kind of raw flesh; they invariably either boil, roast or smoke it . . . Some cut long steaks from the flesh of the thighs, legs and arms; others prefer the hands and feet; and although the great majority do not eat the head, I have come across more than one tribe which prefers this to any other part. Almost all use some part of the intestines on account of the fat they contain.' He complained that he and fellow Europeans were unable to buy meat in the markets for fear it might be human flesh.

The Reverend W. Holman Bentley, in his *Pioneering on the Congo*, wrote of the cannibals: 'They could not understand the objections raised to the practice. "You eat fowls and goats, and we eat men; why not? What is the difference?" The son of Matabwiki, chief of Liboko, when asked whether he had ever eaten human flesh, said: "Ah! I wish that I could eat everyone on earth!"'

Bentley reported that while cannibalism was rife in the Congo, it was even worse on the Nobangi, where tribes 'kept and fattened slaves for butchery as we do cattle and poultry'.

Another missionary, Grenfell, observed that the Bambala tribe regarded as a special delicacy flesh which had been buried for days and was crawling with maggots. And although the women of the tribe were forbidden to eat human flesh, they found ways of getting around the taboo.

An artist named Herbert Ward, who travelled in the Congo, wrote of watching natives eat human flesh. He remarked: 'Probably the most inhuman practice of all is to be met with among the tribes who deliberately hawk the victim piecemeal whilst still alive. Incredible as it may appear, captives are led from place to place in order that individuals may have the opportunity of indicating, by external marks on the body, the portions they desire to acquire. The marks are generally made by means of coloured clay . . . The astounding stoicism of the victims who thus witness the bargaining for their limbs piecemeal, is only equalled by the callousness with which they walk forward to meet their fate.'

Those tribes who were cannibals could be recognized from their practice of filing their teeth to sharp points. Lewis Cotlow, whose book *Zanzabuku* was published in 1957, told of how a German ethnologist wanted to buy human skulls to take home for research purposes but: 'He was disappointed to find that most of the skulls had been shattered – so that the Mangbetu gourmands could get at the brains: a great delicacy.' Cotlow makes the insightful point that: 'The Mangbetu ate human flesh because they raised no cattle.' Both the Zulu and Masai tribes who raised cattle had no record of cannibalism.

In a book published in 1956, H. C. Engert, writing about a trip he made through Central Africa after the Second World War, relates how he met a Danish traveller who told him that he and his party were in the northern part of the Congo when they ran short of food. They bought a stew from a village. 'The flesh was very tender,' the Dane said. After the meal he asked the village elder where the meat had come from, and received the answer: 'It was a woman belonging to the village.'

It is certain that cannibalism existed in the Congo, Uganda and Kenya up until fairly recently, and may still be practised. But it is important to remember that these tribes did not distinguish between animal and human flesh. It was a pragmatic attitude: meat was meat. Even the death of a family member was not so much a cause for mourning as a restocking of the larder, since many tribes ate their dead. With reverence, one hopes. Idi Amin, when he was not busy feeding his victims to the crocodiles, ate pieces of them. But his was the contempt for the individual human life displayed by all tyrants.

Sierra Leone, in West Africa, was the home of the Leopard People, an exclusive clan similar to the Hamatsas of the Kwakiutl Indians. There were the same harsh initiation rites, and the same privileges. A candidate for membership had first to seek out a medicine man or priest of the cult and make his request to join. If his application was approved, he would be told to take a certain road until he met up with a group of Leopard Men. They would vet him.

As a sign of their approval they would give the inititiate a leopard knife: a huge knife with a double-pronged point which was razor-sharp. He then took an oath which meant his death if he ever revealed the secrets of the cult. After three days of seclusion, the party sought out a victim to eat. That act sealed the inititiate's membership. The priest leading a particular group always carried his 'medicine' with him in a box: the flesh of a child who had died at birth.

The party of Leopard Men, usually five or six in number, would go around the various villages, begging for a victim. They might ask a man to give them his brother or sister. Traditionally, the request was denied, but this was a mere formality. No one ever refused the Leopard Men. They would hint loudly that a sacrifice was needed for the good of the tribe . . .

Once a victim had been selected, the Leopard Men would go into the jungle nearby and spend the night roaring like leopards until daybreak. Then one of them, chosen for his bravery, would don the skin of a leopard and, armed with his leopard knife, he would attack and kill the victim, dragging him to the rest of the waiting party, who would cut the body up into four quarters, after which the heart, liver and intestines of the victim would be carefully examined. Once certified satisfactory, the victim was eaten. The face was always cut away from the skull to prevent identification of the victim.

There was obviously some element of witchcraft among the Leopard Men. After the feast, they made an effigy of the victim from banana leaves and sticks, which they set on a pole. A piece of skin from the victim's forehead was placed on the effigy and fat from his kidneys was rubbed on it. Then it was presented to the father or mother of the victim, who had in fact connived at their child's death.

4

AMAZON MENUS

When they want an exotic location for an adventure movie, film makers often pick the Amazon region of South America. We have visited the Americas before, to examine the Aztecs and the Kwakiutl Indians, but those people lived in relatively hospitable places. The Amazon region is a vast and inaccessible place, three million square miles of jungle and crocodile-infested rivers, which remains today much as it did in prehistoric times. Many an explorer – Colonel Fawcett among others – has been swallowed up in its interior.

And perhaps 'swallowed up' is an apt term, since cannibals existed here too. This was one place which the missionaries avoided. A few brave souls did try to establish missions, but were eaten for their pains. What little we know about the Amazon region comes from the reports of intrepid explorers. A. H. Keane of the Royal Geographical Society wrote of his experiences along the Amazon just after the turn of the century:

> The Amajuacas of the Ucayali, near the old Peruvian frontier, have been over and over again converted to Christianity, each time relapsing and murdering the evangelists. The Cashibos, also of the Ucayali, eat their aged parents, but perhaps more from religious sentiment than from cruelty . . . It was the practice of the Cocomas of the Hualaga to eat their dead relatives and to swallow their ground-up bones in fermented drinks, on the plea that it was better to be inside a warm friend than buried in the cold earth.

The Amazon region was home to the head-hunters, summed up in the Latin phrase: *homo homini lupus erat* – man was wolf to his fellow men. Alfred Russel Wallace, credited with having discovered the principle of natural selection at the same time as Darwin, had travelled extensively in the Amazon jungles and left us an account of the funeral practices of the tribes in the region.

The dead are almost always buried in their houses, with their trinkets upon them. They are buried the same day they die, the parents and relatives keeping up a constant mourning and lamentation over the body . . . about a month after their funeral the corpse is disinterred, which is then much decomposed, and put in a great pan over the fire till all the volatile parts are driven off with a most horrible odour, leaving only a black, carbonaceous mass, which is then pounded into a fine powder and mixed in several large vats filled with caxiri. This is then drunk by the assembled company till all is finished. They believe that thus the virtues of the deceased will be transmitted to the drinkers.

H. W. Bates, writing in 1863, describes life upon the River Jufari, a large tributary of the Amazon near Brazil's border with Venezuela. 'They are a fierce, indomitable people. They are also cannibals. Navigation upon the Jauari is rendered impossible on account of the Majeronas lying in wait on its bank to intercept and murder all travellers – especially whites.'

He recalled how two friends had set off by canoes, only to be killed with arrows, then roasted and eaten. Almost all regions in the Amazon contained Indian tribes who used bows and arrows to despatch their victims, save for pygmy tribes, who used the blow-pipe with poisoned darts.

To the explorer, the vast, steaming humid jungles were a trap full of poisonous snakes and predatory animals; but foremost among them was man the flesh-eater.

5
MAN-EATERS OF THE ISLANDS

The South Sea Islands, lying in the south Pacific Ocean between the equator and the Tropic of Capricorn, have long enjoyed a romantic reputation which for the most part was undeserved. Tropical paradises they may have been, with their swaying palm trees and golden sands. Tahiti was home to the French Impressionist painter Paul Gauguin, and had been visited by the *Bounty* prior to the mutiny on that ship. But the islands had a darker side. They contained the species *Homo sapiens* . . .

It was among the Melanesians – the inhabitants of the islands west of the International Date Line – that the practice of cannibalism lasted longest, and in New Guinea the natives ate human flesh as recently as the Second World War. Many Japanese soldiers ended up in their cooking pots.

Fijians had a long tradition of cannibalism, and the tale of Robinson Crusoe, relating how he hid in fear of cannibals visiting his island, is not far short of the truth. Missionaries to Africa may have bemoaned their fate, but Fiji was possibly the worst posting that any young missionary could get. There was far more chance of being eaten than of gaining converts.

On 22 November 1836 a young missionary wrote back to England: *An Appeal to the Sympathy of the Christian Public on Behalf of the Cannibal Feegeeans*.

It read:

Men and Brethren. To your sympathy this Appeal is made,

39

and your help is implored on behalf of a most interesting but deeply depraved people, the inhabitants of a group of islands called Feegee, little known to the civilized world except for the extreme danger to which vessels touching at them are exposed, from the murderous propensities of the islanders, and for the horrid CANNIBALISM to which they are addicted, in which abomination they exceed the New Zealanders themselves.

In Feegee cannibalism is not an occasional but a constant practice; not indulged in from a species of horrid revenge, but from an absolute preference for human flesh over all other food.

We spare you the details of a cannibal feast; the previous murders, the mode of *cooking* human beings, the assembled crowd of all ranks, all ages, both sexes. Chiefs and people, men women and children, anticipating the feast with horrid glee. The actual feast. The attendants bringing into the circle BAKED HUMAN BEINGS – not one, nor two, nor ten – but twenty, thirty, forty, fifty at a single feast! We have heard on credible authority of 200 human beings being thus devoured on these occasions. The writer of this APPEAL has himself conversed with persons who have seen forty or fifty eaten at a single sitting – eaten without anything like disgust; eaten indeed with a high relish! . . . such is the indomitable appetite of the FEEGEEANS for human flesh, that individuals have been known to rob the graves of their deceased children . . .

The missionary naturally hoped to change the habits of the natives with Christian exhortation, but this was doomed to failure. The fact was, as anthropologist A. P. Rice wrote:

Within the Fiji Islands group, cannibalism is one of the established institutions; it is one of the elements of the Fijians' social structure, and is regarded as a refinement which should, and indeed must, be cultivated to become a 'gentleman'. Flesh-eating is a definite part of the Fijians' religion, but they delight in human flesh for its own sake. For example, there is a record of a man living in Ruwai who actually killed his wife, with whom he had been living contentedly . . . and ate her. He agreed that this act was the result of his extreme fondness for human flesh.

The Reverend David Cargill wrote an account in 1838 of the ceremony connected with cannibalism. It must have been read in London with horror.

Some of the circumstances connected with the immolation of human victims are most revolting and diabolical. The passions of the people during the performance of these horrible rites seem inflamed by a fiendish ferocity . . . the victim is selected from among the inhabitants of a distant territory, or is procured by negotiation from a tribe not related to the persons about to sacrifice. The victim is kept for some time and is supplied with an abundance of food, that he may become fat.

When about to be immolated, he is made to sit on the ground with his feet under his thighs and his hands placed before him. He is then bound so that he cannot move a limb or joint. In this posture he is placed on stones heated for the occasion (and some of them are red-hot), and then covered with leaves and earth, to be roasted alive. When cooked, he is taken out of the oven and, his face and other parts being painted black, that he may resemble a living man ornamented for a feast or for war, he is carried to the temple of the gods . . . and is offered as a propitiatory sacrifice.

Afterwards, of course, the crowd ate the sacrifice.

The Feegeeans eat human flesh not merely from a principle of revenge, nor from necessity, but from choice. Captives and strangers are frequently killed and eaten. The natives of Thakanndrove kidnap men, women and children to glut their appetite for human flesh; it is said that, as if they were living hyenas, they disinter dead bodies, after they have been two or three days under the ground; and that, having washed them in the sea, they roast and devour them.

Cargill kept a day-to-day diary which makes vivid reading.

41

October 31st, 1839, Thursday. This morning we witnessed a shocking spectacle. Twenty dead bodies of men, women and children were brought to Rewa as a present from Tanoa. They were distributed among the people to be cooked and eaten. They were dragged about in the water and on the beach. The children amused themselves by sporting with and mutilating the body of a little girl. A crowd of men and women maltreated the body of a grey-haired old man and that of a young woman. Human entrails were floating down the river in front of the mission premises . . .

Later, he found a human head in his garden.

The head had been thrown into our garden during the night, with the intention, no doubt, of annoying us and shocking our feelings . . . These poor victims of war were brought from Verata, and were killed by the Bau people. 260 human beings were killed and brought away by the victors to be roasted and eaten.

A missionary named Jaggar reported back to London in 1844: 'One of the servants of the king a few months ago ran away. She was soon, however, brought back to the king's house. There, at the request of the queen, her arm was cut off below the elbow and cooked for the king, who ate it *in her presence* . . . The girl, now a woman, is still living.'

Jaggar related how the Bau people cooked and ate their victims.

The men doomed to death were made to dig a hole in the earth for the purpose of making a native oven, and were then required to cut firewood to *roast their own bodies*. They were then directed to go and wash, and afterwards, to make a cup from a banana-leaf. This, from opening a vein in each man, was soon filled with blood. This blood was then drunk *in the presence of the sufferers*, by the Kamba people.

Seru, the Bau chief, then had their arms and legs cut off, cooked and eaten, some of the flesh being presented to them. He then ordered a fish-hook to be put into their tongues, which were then drawn out as far as possible before being cut off. These were roasted and eaten, to the taunts of: 'We are eating your tongues!' As life in the victims was still not extinct, an incision was made into the side of each man, and his bowels taken out. This soon terminated their sufferings in this world.

A traveller named Alfred St Johnston published his memoirs, *Camping Among Cannibals* in 1883. He wrote: 'The expression *long pig* is not a phrase invented by Europeans but is one frequently used by the Fijians, who looked upon a corpse as ordinary butcher's meat. They call a human body *puaka balava* – "long pig" – in contradistinction to *puaka dina* – real pig.'

Many observers reported that the Fijians preserved human flesh in salt, and carried it about with them to chew, as Europeans chewed tobacco. St Johnston confirmed this habit, and took a sanguine view of cannibalism. If it was not excusable, for him it was at least understandable. He wrote: 'The Fijians loved human flesh for its own sake, and did not merely eat a slain enemy out of revenge. Probably the absence of any animal they could eat gave rise to the custom . . . ' This was a good point. The only animal native to the islands was the rat, the pig not being introduced until the eighteenth century.

St Johnston continued: 'The crew of every boat that was wrecked upon these shores was killed and eaten in some parts. Often a man would order to be clubbed some man or woman that he considered would be good for cooking, his plea being that his "back tooth was aching" and only human flesh could cure it. Such was the absolute right of a man over his wife that he could kill and eat her if he wished . . . ' He went on to describe the Fijian's 'craving' for human flesh, and said that some chiefs were such gluttons that some of them had consumed hundreds of human bodies. He also reported: 'So delicious was human flesh held to be, that the highest praise that could be given to other food was to say: "It is as good as *bakolo*.'" (A. P. Rice quoted the case of a chief known to have eaten over nine hundred people.)

Felix Maynard was a French surgeon who was serving aboard a ship attached to a whaling fleet operating in the South Pacific. He recorded his experiences in a book: 'Captain Morell, the American skipper of whom I have already spoken, came near to being the victim of an ambush in the Fiji Islands. He lost fourteen of his companions. After regaining his ship, he said, he saw the savages cutting up the members of his poor sailors while they were still alive, and more than one of them saw his own arm or leg roasted and devoured before his death.'

A. P. Rice made a long study of cannibalism in the Polynesian islands and became convinced that in their particular circumstances, cannibalism was not an unnatural practice: 'It was a most natural appetite for good red meat. Natural man is carnivorous. Meat is his natural food.' It was the equivalent of saying, to paraphrase Rousseau, that: 'Man is born a cannibal . . . It is civilization which places him in chains . . .'

Savage as the Fijians undoubtedly were, their islands had a beauty and charm of their own. Other islands, although geographically in the South Seas, were not at all pleasant or pretty places. They were grim and forbidding, with thick jungles and inhospitable climates. Such were New Britain, New Ireland, the Solomons, Vanuatu and New Caledonia. They are part of a long chain of islands which stretches for some two thousand miles, and cannibalism had a long tradition among them. The first Spaniards to land there were horrified to be offered lumps of human flesh as a welcome offering . . .

Early missionaries tried hard to get the custom outlawed, but were threatened with being eaten themselves for their pains. Various anthropologists who visited the islands noted that the natives preferred black flesh to white, and boiled it before cooking to remove hair, just as they scalded pigs to remove the bristles. Another custom

44

noted was that if a chief died, it was obligatory for every member of the tribe to consume a piece of him.

Among Samoans, cannibalism had more of a religious element than among the greedy Fijians, and they ate human flesh for either ritual or revenge motives, rather than from gluttony.

Captain Cook discovered Hawaii in 1778 and was to meet his death there at the hands of the natives. Contemporary accounts of his death seem to bear out suspicions that flesh-eating was practised in Hawaii, too.

A canoe paddled by two natives came out to the ship and the natives presented the crew with a lump of flesh weighing about nine pounds and wrapped in cloth. They explained that it was all that remained of Captain Cook, and expressed their sorrow.

Certainly cannibalism was practised on Easter Island, that place of the giant carved statues; and in the Marquesas bodies were spit-roasted on long poles which passed through the mouth and anus.

Perhaps the most brutal of all the island was New Guinea, parts of which remain unexplored and unmapped to this day. Half of the island used to be ruled by the Dutch, the other half by Britain and Australia. All three civilized nations tried hard to eradicate cannibalism. In 1912 J. H. P. Murray, the Lieutenant-Governor and Chief Judicial Officer of Papua New Guinea, wrote: 'Certain tribes here like human flesh and do not see why they should not eat it. Indeed, I have never been able to give a convincing answer to a native who says to me: "Why should I not eat human flesh?"'

It appears from all the accounts that in New Guinea the victims were boiled rather than roasted – the taste was said to resemble that of pork – and the motive for eating human flesh, apart from a need for red meat, was a strong strand of revenge against slain enemies.

In Borneo, the third largest island in the world, cannibalism seems to have been practised mainly for the sake of obtaining human heads. The Dyaks collected heads, extracting the brains for eating, but when asked why they ate human flesh, they replied: 'If we do not eat of warrior's flesh, how can we hope ourselves to become as fearless as they?'

There seems to have been a strong religious motive for head-hunting, to promote the well-being of the tribal crops and cattle. The head was believed to contain the soul, or *toh*, and thus the Dyaks were soul-hunters . . .

6

CANNIBALISM IN THE ANTIPODES

Most of Australia's inhabitants – who number little more than the population of London – live on the fringe of the continent, on its shoreline. The vast interior of some three million square miles remains bleak and inhospitable. Yet the Aborigine has lived in the interior for thousands of years, with no fixed dwellings nor any real development in agriculture. Together with Eskimos, Aborigines are the nearest people we have today to Stone-Age men. There has been little evolution since prehistoric times, and they were the most primitive race on earth when Captain Cook first came across them. Now barely fifty thousand of them remain in existence.

Colin Simpson, in his *Adam in Ochre* (1938) tells us that in hard summers when food was scarce, all newborn children were eaten by the Kaura tribe in the region of Adelaide. Among many tribes it was observed that flesh-eating was a sign of respect for the dead. 'We eat him because we knew him and were fond of him,' as one tribesman explained.

Some tribes, the Ngarigo among them, ate slain enemies as a gesture of contempt, eating the flesh of their hands and feet while shouting loud insults at the people killed.

In Central and Western Australia, young men used to go through an initiation ceremony where they had to drink human blood. Blood was considered both sacred and strength-giving. A. P. Elkin, one-time Professor of Anthropology at the University of Sydney, wrote at length about the initiation rites of the Aborigine, pointing out that it was customary for young men to spend a good deal of their seclusion in *pairs*, so assisting one another to obtain food. He wrote: 'In nearly all the tribes from the west to the east, and from the north to the south, at some point in the initiation series a blood rite is performed. It consists of anointing the newly initiated with arm-blood fom the older men, or else giving them some of this to drink. The older men also anoint themselves, or each other, and drink blood. This blood is sacred; there is a secret name for it, and it is usually associated with some mythical hero's act.' The important thing to note here is that the drinking of human blood takes on the nature of a *sacramental rite*.

Aborigines smoked the bodies of the dead over their camp fires. It helped to preserve the meat under the hot sun. In his book *Whispering Wind* (1957) Kyle-Little reported:

> The Liverpool River natives did not kill a man for food. They ate human flesh largely from superstitious beliefs. If they killed a worthy man in battle they ate his heart, believing that they would inherit his valour and power. They ate his brain because they knew it represented the seat of his knowledge. If they killed a fast man, they ate part of his legs to acquire his speed.

The Aborigines lived by an elaborate system of magical beliefs, which they had inherited from the 'dream time' before the coming of the European. They had sacred chants which they sang at important ceremonies, and their cave paintings reveal the same obsession with their gods. The most widely known of their beliefs is perhaps the 'boning to death' of an enemy. Among the Wonkonguru tribe in particular, the pointing bone was called the *wirra garoo*. It was a bone with marks around it at regular intervals, with human hair at one end as a decorative motif. Once pointed at an enemy, and the magical death-song sung into it, the intended victim would fall ill and gradually die. As the bone pointer burned more of the bone, the victim became more ill; when the last segment was burned, he fell dead. This has been observed by scientists and is known to have occurred when the two men, the pointer and the victim, were thousands of miles apart and with no possibility that the victim could have known of the sentence passed upon him. It remains inexplicable, except in terms of magic.

The Aborigine, then, was a cannibal almost from necessity, and certainly from a religious motive. As E. O. James wrote in his *Origins of Sacrifice* (1933), 'Among the native tribes of Australia the bodies of those who fall in battle, honoured chiefs, and new-born infants, are frequently consumed to obtain their qualities, just as in the Torres Straits the tongue and sweat of a slain enemy are imbibed to get his bravery.'

New Zealand has about the same number of Maoris as Australia has Aborigines, but since New Zealand has a population only a quarter that of her neighbour, they form a much higher proportion of the population.

The Maoris are an interesting mix. While physically they are Polynesian, they have the traditions of Melanesia and seem to have more in common, culturally, with the Fiji Islanders than the Aborigines. Where they came from remains a mystery; many anthropologists believe that they hopped from island to island to reach New Zealand, perhaps originating from India or Central Asia. Whatever their origin, they proved to be far more cannibal-minded than the Aborigines.

Captain Cook was horrified to find the natives eating human flesh in New Zealand when he landed there in 1768. He was engaged in charting the coastline for the Admiralty in the *Endeavour*. The ship had first visited the Society Islands and Tahiti, and Cook and his officers were unprepared for what they discovered in New Zealand.

Captain Cook kept a careful day-to-day diary, and his *Journals* describe the grim discovery made by his officers.

Calm light airs from the north all day on the 23rd November hindered us from putting to sea as intended. In the afternoon some of the officers went on shore to amuse themselves among the natives, where they saw the head and bowels of a youth, who had been lately killed, lying on the beach, and the heart stuck on a forked stick which was fixed on the head of one of the largest canoes. One of the gentlemen bought the head and brought it on board, where a piece of the flesh was broiled and eaten by one of the natives, before all of the officers and most of the men . . . The sight of the head . . . struck me with horror and filled my mind with indignation against these cannibals.

Dr Felix Maynard, writing just over a century ago, related the case of Touai, a New Zealand chief who was brought to England in 1818 and lived in London for a long time, becoming accepted in society. But even after many years: 'He confessed in his moments of nostalgia that what he most regretted in the country from which he was absent was the feast of human flesh, the feast of victory. He was weary of eating English beef; he claimed that there was a great analogy between the flesh of the pig and that of man. This last declaration he made before a sumptuously served table. The flesh of women and children was to him and his fellow-countrymen the most delicious, while certain Maoris preferred that of a man of fifty, and that of a black rather than a white. His countrymen, Touai said, never ate the flesh raw, and preserved the fat of the rump for the purpose of dressing their sweet potatoes.'

Maynard went on: 'Usually, after a fight, they commence by devouring the bodies of the oldest and most courageous warriors, those most completely tattooed, leaving the corpses of the younger men aside, those that were novices in warfare, even though their flesh be more appetizing. Thus, before all, the victors value the assimilation, the appropriation of the life and courage of the most celebrated warriors, *however thin and fleshless they might be.*' Maynard adds: 'Considered from this point of view, cannibalism is almost excusable among barbarous peoples.'

Maynard described Maori cannibal feasts, noting that the brain was particularly esteemed, and that the bones of a chief were carefully collected and made into fish-hooks, arrow-points, needles, and even clothes-pegs. He stated his belief that the Maori custom of cutting off an enemy's head and raising it up so that they might drink the warm blood running from it was done in order to inherit the soul of the foe.

Though the New Zealanders do not conceal their cannibalism, their chiefs sometimes endeavour to excuse themselves for it. 'The fish of the sea eat one another,' they say; 'the large fish eat the small ones, the small ones eat insects; dogs eat men and men eat dogs, while dogs eat one another; the birds of the air also prey upon one another; finally, the gods devour other gods. Why, among enemies, should *we* not eat one another?'

In *The Maori Race* (1904) Edward Tregear recorded:

After battle comes the terrible and revolting episode of the cannibal feast. Prisoners taken in the fight were slain in cold blood, except those reserved for slavery – a mark of still greater contempt than being killed for food.

In a day near our own it is recorded that a chief named Wherowhero ordered 250 prisoners of the Taranaki people to be brought to him for slaughter. He sat on the ground and the prisoners were brought to him one by one to receive the blow of the chief's *mere* – a weapon till lately in the possession of his son, the late Maori 'King'. After he had killed the greater number of them he said, 'I am tired. Let the rest live.' So the remainder passed into slavery . . . One of the latest cannibal feasts of consequence was held at Ohariu, near Wellington, when 150 people of the Maupoko tribe went into the ovens . . . I was shown a beach on the

Chatham Islands on which the bodies of eighty Moriori women were laid side by side, each with an impaling stake driven into the abdomen. It is difficult for one not accustomed to savage warfare to note how shockingly callous and heartless this desecration of the human body made the actors in these terrible scenes.

We do have an eyewitness account of a cannibal feast from a rather disreputable Captain Stewart, master of the trading brig *Elizabeth*. He agreed to smuggle a Maori chief and his warriors to an island where their enemies lived. He took over a hundred warriors on board, landing them on the beach of the island in the early hours. Soon the canoes began returning with prisoners, who were held in the hold. Rather sanctimoniously the captain reported: 'None of those prisoners were killed or cooked aboard the ship.'

Instead, the victims were cooked on shore in the Maori custom: they were placed in holes some two feet deep containing red-hot stones, and covered with earth and leaves. The captain *did* transport one hundred baskets of flesh, each containing the equivalent of one human being, for his Maori friends, then watched as they disposed of the still-living prisoners on the beach.

The warriors, entirely naked, their long black hair, although matted with human gore, yet flowing partially in the wind; in the left hand a human head, and in the right a bayoneted musket held by the middle of the barrel. This, with a song, the terrible expression of which can only be imagined by being heard, did they dance around their wretched victims, every now and then approaching them with gestures, threatening death under its most horrible forms of lingering torture ... The tables were laid. About a hundred baskets of potatoes, a large supply of green vegetables, and equal quantities of whale-blubber and human flesh, constituted the awful menu ...

Daniel Henry Sheridan was a trader who witnessed a

vendetta between two tribes, the Waikato and the Taranaki. He wrote an account of what he saw in a letter home, which survives for posterity:

The principal part of the prisoners that day were cripples, women and children; the remainder making their escape as well as their weak state would allow . . . A party of the enemy were employed in despatching as many as would be sufficient for the evening's meal; their slaves getting the ovens ready, and the remainder went in search of more prey, which they found to the number of *twelve hundred*. On the 23rd they commenced the slaughter of the prisoners that were taken alive. They were crammed into huts, well guarded, the principal chief executioner, with a sharp tomahawk in his hand, ready to receive them. They were then called out one by one. Those that had well tattooed heads had their heads cut off on a block, the body quartered and hung upon fences that were erected for the purpose. Those with indifferent heads received one blow, and were then dragged to a hole to bleed. The young children, and grown-up lads, were cut down the belly and then roasted on sticks before the fires . . .

Sheridan estimated that some three hundred people had been eaten in all.

He went on to relate what he saw in the settlement, adding the pious comment:

Oh, what a scene for a man of Christian feeling to behold, dead bodies strewed about the settlement in every direction . . . They got sixteen bodies, besides a great number that were half-roasted, and dug several up out of the graves, half decayed, which they also ate. Another instance of their depravity was to make a musket ramrod red-hot, enter it into the lower part of the victim's belly and let it run upwards, and then make a slight incision in a vein to let his blood run gradually for them to drink . . .

He ended his letter thus: 'I must here conclude, being very scanty of paper; for which reason, columns of the disgraceful conduct of these cannibals remain unpenned by Daniel Henry Sheridan.'

These 'disgraceful cannibals' are today as civilized as the whites among whom they live. They have not, like the Aborigine, remained a basically primitive and nomadic people. They still perform their tribal dances on ceremonial occasions, but they retain only a vestige of their former culture.

7
MODERN CANNIBALISM

Leaving cannibalism from necessity aside, there can be no doubt that cannibalism is still practised in some parts of the world to this day. A few years ago a scandal involving a French government minister and Emperor Bokassa, head of an African state, whose coronation cost millions at a time when his people were starving, and the curious present of valuable diamonds, made headlines in the world's press and nearly toppled a government. What was also reported, but in smaller type, was that the former chef to Bokassa revealed that the self-proclaimed 'emperor' kept his fridge well-stocked with strips of human flesh. Idi Amin, too, was a reputed flesh-eater.

A little thought gives a clue to this kind of behaviour. Previous chapters have made mention of cannibalism as a gesture of contempt. Now, if a man is an absolute tyrant, with absolute power over the fate of his people, what is the ultimate crime he can inflict upon them? Simply raping and killing them is not enough. It leaves behind bodies and bones which might become a martyr's relics, a shrine to the opposition.

Eating one's opponents is the ultimate gesture of contempt, since not only is the tyrant disposing of the evidence of his crime by eating it, he is absorbing into himself his foes, and turning them literally into excrement. One is reminded of the savage philosophy expressed by De Sade: 'Simply to deprive them of their life is not enough. A method must be found of depriving them of their *second* life.'

The most recent *social and organized* form of cannibalism was displayed by the Mau Mau of East Africa during the troubles in Kenya during the 1950s. The Mau Mau was an African army which fought a war aimed at independence from colonial rulers, a war fought against British soldiers. Today we would undoubtedly call them 'freedom fighters' and so on. But the methods they practised were as old as man himself – and just as tyrannical.

The term 'Mau Mau' was simply another name for the old Kenya Central Association, just as Sinn Fein is the political wing of the IRA. But when the Mau Mau was formed as a fighting army, it adopted a curious mix of British nomenclature and primitive African customs. The members were called 'soldiers', and they had the ranks of any army, from captain up to field marshal. But they also had elaborate and disgusting rituals to ensure the loyalty of the members.

Each recruit had to take an oath of loyalty and secrecy, and the ritual was made as religio-magical as it could be to ensure that the recruit kept secret the names of fellow members. It was a kind of brainwashing so that any captured Mau Mau kept his mouth shut even when questioned under penalty of death. It worked because the man was more frightened of his tribal chief than he was of any British soldier.

The oaths had eight levels. Ione Leigh, in his book, *In the Shadow of the Mau Mau* (1954) described the rites:

> The first oath, which is the mildest, is taken in a darkened room where an arch of sugar-cane or banana-leaves has been erected. In an atmosphere of gloom, the candidate divests himself of all European articles, such as watches, shoes and clothing. Rings of Igoka grass are then placed over his head and wrists, and standing naked before the arch he takes the oath. Seven *sodum* apples are included in the ritual to bring misfortune to him if he breaks the oath; the eyes of a slaughtered sheep, pierced with *mugai* thorns, also denote the fate of those who break their vows.
>
> A 'banana-bell' which has been hollowed out and filled

with a mixture of blood and earth, is rotated seven times around his head, after which a stick of wild hibiscus is dipped into the blood and put to his lips. He licks the blood and bites the chest of the slaughtered sheep seven times. Blood is then drawn from his arm and mixed with the sheep's blood, which all initiates must drink. This forms the 'blood-brother-hood'. Live cats and dogs and certain parts of human bodies are sometimes nailed to Mau Mau altars.

The oaths became progressively more violent in nature as the recruit passed up the ranks. Among the vows which the initiate had to make was one pledging that whenever he killed a European he would cut off the head, extract the eyeballs, and drink the liquid from them.

For the fourth oath, which is usually taken before an African becomes a Captain in the Mau Mau army, a dead body has to be provided. At the ceremony the fingers of the dead man are bent seven times, and his eyes pricked seven times. A Major takes the fifth oath. He is required to bite the brain of a dead African seven times. For a Brigadier, the brain of a *white* man has to be provided. The candidate proceeds to eat seven pieces of it. A General, who takes the seventh oath, is required to eat, besides the brain, the wrist-bones of a white man, broken up and mixed with his excrement and blood. For the last oath, a man and a child must first be killed. The heart of the child is cut from its body, and pricked seven times with a nail; the brains and blood of the dead man are then mixed with the blood of the oath-taker, and all members are required to drink the draught.

Of course, it was never as simple as all that. In order to make the rituals more mysterious and mind-bending, various other factors were introduced, such as sexual perversions with various animals – rams, dogs, sheep, goats, and so on. Documents regarding the oath-taking ceremonies of the Mau Mau are still kept under lock and key at the Foreign Office. They are considered to be too disgusting for ordinary eyes.

Today, missionaries point with pride to the civilizing

result of their work, with cannibalism eradicated over all the globe and the practice consigned to the obscurity of the dark and degraded past. It is something not to be talked about.

But is it possible that somewhere in the world, in some remote corner of New Guinea or Africa, men still eat human flesh?

We know that in New York and Tokyo men still eat flesh, but we call them 'criminals' and prosecute them in courts of law. But these are very isolated cases indeed, the acts of aberrant individuals.

Even so, it appears inconceivable that cannibalism, an act so intricately bound up with man's common heritage, and part of his diet for the best part of a million years, is not still carried on somewhere on the planet on a regular basis. And given what we know about human nature, any future catastrophe, such as a nuclear holocaust, would bring the old habit of flesh-eating right back into prominence.

PART II: CANNIBALISM FROM NECESSITY

1
SEYE THE BANDIT

'Necessity' is a rather loose term, as will be seen from the following accounts. Necessity can soon become a justified craving . . .

The first such cannibal in modern times we have on record is Blaise Ferrage Seye, who appeared to be something of a misanthrope. Born in Cessan, near Comminges, in 1757, Seye proved from an early age that he was no misogynist. A stone mason by trade, he spent his spare time seducing the local women, to such effect that an angry and powerful husband forced him to flee for his life into the mountains.

Having made a home for himself in a cave, he now had the problem of survival in a hostile terrain. At first he raided the local villages, stealing cattle and poultry, and, on occasion, young girls. He frightened off any would-be pursuers by firing his fowling-piece at them and, at least once, when a girl attempted to escape from him, he shot her dead and then raped her still-warm body.

For three years he lived as a bandit, a terror to the local populace. Procuring animals for food became ever more difficult, as farmers banded together to protect their flocks and there was nothing in the mountains worth hunting. And so Seye hit upon a simple expedient to solve his dietary needs: he began hunting men.

Soon he began to *prefer* human flesh to, say, the stringy and coarse meat of an old goat, and the hunt took on a whole new dimension. There was the thrill of the chase, the pleasure of the rape, and then the satisfaction of eating the object of it all. The men he captured he cooked and ate, but women captives had different uses.

In 1782 he was captured when a fellow crook tipped off the police as to the location of his cave. The twenty-five-year-old Seye was first broken on the wheel and then exposed to die on the gibbet. He displayed his misanthropic streak when he gazed with enormous disdain at the huge crowd which had gathered to watch his execution.

2
PIERCE THE PLUNDERER

Alexander Pierce had been transported to the colonies, and found himself imprisoned at the harsh convict camp in Van Dieman's Land (Tasmania). He and five other convicts managed to escape by boat in 1823, and safely reached the mainland. But it had been an exhausting trip, and one of the party remarked that he was so hungry he could eat a man. An unfortunate choice of words, as it turned out.

That night, as he lay in an exhausted sleep, the other members of the party killed him, then cut out his heart, which they fried and ate.

The escaped convicts discovered that life outside the camp was grim. There were no regular meals – no matter how badly cooked. One by one the members of the party died, the others eating them in turn for survival. The fourth one was in a bad state, ready to drop, but he was helped on his way with a blow from an axe. He was duly eaten.

Now only Pierce and one other convict remained, both eyeing each other nervously. The other man took to carrying an axe about with him, strapping it to his body while he slept. But he *had* to sleep, and it was then that Pierce murdered him, braining him with a chunk of rock. He then took his axe and hacked off his limbs to cook.

Soon after eating the last surviving convict, Pierce himself was recaptured. A year later he again escaped from the convict settlement, along with another man. The other man was simply a walking food parcel, so far as

Pierce was concerned. A couple of days after the escape, Pierce killed him and partially ate him.

Again Pierce was recaptured. He showed the soldiers who had tracked him down the remains of the human meat he had stored away. The soldiers noted with some curiosity that the meat and fish which Pierce had stolen from the prison for his break-out were still in his pack, uneaten. These were obviously his 'emergency' rations. Inexplicably, Pierce was not executed for his crimes and died in prison.

3

THE DONNER PARTY

The story of the Donner party is part of the American heritage, a true story which has become interwoven with the legend of the Old West.

Pioneers wanting to settle in the West had to follow a two thousand-mile-long trail from Missouri to California, and the greatest barrier on the long trek was not the marauding Indians, but the high peaks of the Sierra Nevada. They could only be crossed in the spring, when the snow had cleared from its passes, and so there was a season for the wagons full of emigrants. Unfortunately, George Donner, a farmer from Illinois who was leader of an eighty-seven-strong company of men, women and children, had chosen the wrong time of year. He had set out too late.

The party had left in the summer, headed for California – the 'promised land' – travelling in high-wheeled wagons pulled by sturdy oxen. The long and arduous journey across the Nevada and Utah deserts had already cost them five lives – now mute and unposted graves in the sand.

The party was in sight of the mountains, but still on the wrong side of them, travelling up the banks of the Truckee River in Nevada. It was late October 1846, and winter had come early. Snow plumes whipped across the peaks, carried by strong gusting winds. They had to get across, being desperately short of food. Indians had taken many of their cattle, and of the twenty wagons which had begun the journey, only fifteen remained.

George Donner and his wife Tamsen led the way. Following closely behind was Jacob Donner, brother of George, with his wife and children. Lewis Keseberg was a German from Westphalia, hoping for a new life in California with his wife Phillipine and their two small children. There were many other families strung out across miles of hostile terrain, some struggling to keep up.

By 30 October the party had reached Truckee Lake, six thousand feet up the mountains. As a snow blizzard enveloped them, George Donner turned back in his wagon to help the stragglers, some of them five miles behind. Progress became slower and slower as the snow grew deeper and the men weaker. They made camp for the night, knowing that their situation was desperate and that they would have to go on the next day. To turn back would be madness.

They woke in the morning to find themselves buried in ten-foot-deep snowdrifts. It was impossible for the wagons to move, and so the decision was taken that the party would leave the wagons behind and, taking only their most precious possessions, would attempt to cross the summit pass on foot. For four grim days they struggled through the chest-high snow, soaked and freezing, before realising that they were trapped and could not continue.

On 3 November 1846, they gave up and began the trek back to the wagons. Here, and in another camp five miles back, they made camp. Eighty-seven men, women and children, hoping somehow to survive the winter with only a day's supply of food. And yet safety lay only a day's journey across the pass. It was a cruel dilemma.

One party made its camp on the shore of Truckee Lake. Such families as the Kesebergs, the Breens, Reeds and Murphys built and occupied log cabins, making up a community of around sixty people, of whom half were children. Five miles away George Donner and his wife built another camp; their party included twelve children.

At first they lived by killing off oxen and roasting them over camp fires, but it soon became apparent that the threat of starvation was very real.

By 12 November it was obvious that unless drastic measures were taken to bring aid, the surviving members of the party would die. A group of thirteen of the fittest members was selected to cross the summit pass on foot, carrying dried strips of meat for sustenance. This attempt, and another a week later, failed. Sheer exhaustion forced the men back.

It was a time of desperation. It was decided that by using crude snow-shoes, the adults with sufficient strength would make a dash across the mountains to safety. Six weeks of snow blizzards had temporarily ended and the prospects seemed good. On the morning of 16 December a party of ten men, two youths and five young women set out, leaving Lewis Keseberg in charge of the camp. They had heard no word from the Donner camp for weeks, yet it was only five miles away.

It was a journey of heroism and defeat. Two men turned back on the second day. The effects of cold, altitude and hunger made every step a nightmare. On Christmas Day they were caught in another snow storm near the summit. Three of the party were already dead, the rest were in a desperately bad condition, hallucinating from cold and hunger.

William Eddy, a farmer from Illinois, told his companions: 'There is nothing left to eat – but ourselves.' Another member, Patrick Dolan, was already in a coma. Without sustenance he would die. The day after Christmas Dolan was dead. Weeping with grief and emotion, the survivors hacked the flesh from his body and roasted it over a fire. They all ate.

The next to die was twelve-year-old Lemuel Murphy. His married sister Sarah took part in the eating of his body. For three days the party rested. Fifteen had set out. Five were dead, one lost in the snow, and four cooked and packed for the journey which lay ahead. The five remaining men, William Eddy, husband of Sarah Murphy, William Foster, Jay Fosdick and two Indian guides knew this would not be enough.

By the evening of 1 January 1847 the ten survivors had eaten the last of the cooked human flesh which had been their only food for a week. William Foster said bluntly: 'If any of us are going to survive, one of us will have to be killed.' He suggested they should kill the two Indian guides. But William Eddy was appalled by the idea, and secretly warned the two men, who left the camp that night, under cover of darkness. Then Jay Fosdick died, solving the immediate problem – but not for long. As the party staggered onwards, they came across the tracks of the two Indians, who were lying under trees completely exhausted. It was now 9 January. Foster shot both men dead with his pistol.

The double murder caused a split in the group, which separated into two parties. Eddy and three of the women now camped separately from Foster and his two women. Foster had the meat of two Indians to survive on, Eddy and his women had just the dried remains of Fosdick.

Ten days later the survivors lurched into Johnson's ranch, the first settlement in the Sacramento Valley. They were a pitiful sight: half-naked, and with their faces smeared with human blood. They had existed on human flesh for a total of thirty-three days.

The survivors blurted out their horrifying story, and a relief team set out to rescue the Donner party, pushing its way across the Sierras from the Californian side, loaded with supplies of food.

Meanwhile, across the mountains the main party had waited through December and January for news that the rescue mission had been successful, but heard nothing. They feared the worst, and existed by eating their dogs and even the hides which formed the roofs of their shelters. When the relief party from California finally arrived at the camp by Truckee Lake on 18 February, they found a horrifying sight. Bodies lay sprawled out in the snow, dead from starvation. The survivors had been too weak to bury them.

The rescuers decided to take those who were fit enough to get out, and twenty-four emaciated people gathered to make the hazardous journey to safety. The rescuers had to leave behind the dead, and thirty-two men, women and children who would have to wait for a further rescue party. Even worse, the rescuers could not afford to leave them any supplies. Twenty-two of the twenty-four rescued people survived the crossing. But it was what happened to those left behind at Lake Truckee which makes the story so tragic.

When a second rescue party reached the camps on 1 March, they found a terrible silence. In one cabin lay the body of Milt Elliot. His head was untouched, but most of the meat had been stripped from his body. Half-chewed bones lay all around. At the Donner camp things were just as bad. A man came across the snow to the rescuers, calmly carrying the leg of a man. Jacob Donner had been cut into pieces, and his body had kept the party alive. Mrs Jacob Donner had refused to eat the flesh of her husband, but she had cut him up and fed him to her children. At least fifteen bodies had been consumed in this way.

The rescuers assembled the survivors and set off in haste back across the mountain, but on 3 March they were caught in the pass by a severe snow-storm – the worst that winter. The large party huddled around a fire, but soon their food was gone, and what had begun as a rescue attempt had ended in disaster. Two of the fourteen men were dead.

Mary Donner, aged seven, said innocently: 'We'll have to eat the dead people.' Within an hour the corpse of Mrs Elizabeth Graves lay dismembered. Her breasts, heart and liver were cooking over the camp fire, as her one-year-old baby lay beside what remained of his mother. By the time this party was rescued, Mrs Graves and two children had been eaten in this way. The

69

remaining eleven were too shocked to talk about the experience. Adversity had broken the taboo against eating human flesh, but they had to live the rest of their lives with the memory of what they had done.

Back at the camps, the same pattern was repeating itself. Lewis Keseberg had been left with the Donners, and others, to wait for a third rescue attempt. Mrs Donner had loyally refused to be rescued, preferring to stay behind to nurse her husband George, who was dying from a gangrenous arm. Keseberg now had the look of a savage about him; all his European sophistication had vanished. One night he took four-year-old George Foster to bed with him. Next morning the boy was dead. Although the rest suspected murder, Keseberg claimed the boy had died naturally, and he calmly hung the lad upside down to butcher him for eating.

It was 13 March before the final rescue party broke through, to find more of the survivors had died, more had been eaten. It was the last chance of a rescue before spring, but again Mrs Donner refused to leave her dying husband. Eventually it was decided that Mrs Donner would stay behind to nurse her husband, together with Lewis Keseberg, looking after the dying Mrs Murphy, and two more strong survivors were left behind to care for the rest. If they could hang on for another month, when the snows melted, all could be saved.

It was not to be. No sooner had the rescuers departed than the two fit men left behind to look after the rest looted the possessions of the survivors and set off for the pass and safety.

There were no witnesses to what happened next. On 19 March Mrs Murphy died, and Lewis Keseberg kept himself alive by eating her. Five miles away Mrs Donner was nursing her husband, who was close to death. On the afternoon of 26 March, Mrs Donner appeared at Keseberg's cabin. Her husband had died, and now only she and Keseberg remained alive. Mrs Donner's refusal to leave her husband had doomed her.

When on 17 April another rescue party reached the Truckee Lake, they found only Lewis Keseberg alive. There was an immediate suspicion that he had murdered Mrs Donner, since just a month previously she had appeared to be fit and healthy, and clues in his cabin suggested that the blond German had indeed butchered his only remaining companion. Two cauldrons were full of human blood, while fresh liver was frying in a pan. When questioned, Keseberg admitted that Mrs Donner was dead, but said that she had wandered off into the snow and had died from exposure. He was asked: 'What happened to Mrs Donner's body?'

In a thick accent he replied: 'Some of her is there.' He waved a hand to indicate the pan of liver. 'The rest I have eaten. She was the best I have ever tasted.' Although threatened with torture and beaten, and despite the belongings of the dead woman being found in his possession, Keseberg refused to admit to murdering her.

On 25 April the party was ready to leave for safety, taking with them the one survivor from a camp in which forty-two people had died. The snow had melted, revealing the remains of dismembered corpses, but also frozen horse and ox meat. One final question was put to Keseberg: 'When animal meat was available, why did you persist in your diet of human flesh?'

Keseberg replied: 'I tried them, but they were too dry for my taste. Human liver and lights are far more tasty. And as for human brains, well, they make the best soup of all.' This was all the more chilling because the body of George Donner had been discovered with its skull split open and the brains removed.

Of the eighty-seven original members of the Donner party only forty-seven had made it to California. Forty had either died of starvation or had been eaten. Those were not normal times with normal rules of conduct, and although Keseberg was widely regarded as a murderer, he went unpunished. In fact, he had the temerity to sue for slander someone who had accused him of murder.

He won his case, but was awarded a derisory one dollar in damages. In later years Keseberg was to be seen making the rounds of California bars, boasting of his exploits with the Donner party. And he paid this extraordinary tribute to Tamsen Donner: 'She was the healthiest woman I ever ate. I boiled out four pounds of fat from her body.'

In the early 1850s Keseberg opened a steakhouse, advertising that he sold only the finest and tenderest of meat.

4

CANNIBALS AT SEA
The Mignonette Case

Sheer necessity – the need to save one's life – is accepted by Catholic theologians as a justification for cannibalism. But what is the opinion of the law? In the last century the case of the Mignonette survivors excited great public interest, and the legal issue about people eating people appeared to have been settled.

The circumstances of the case were simple enough. An Australian, Mr J. H. Want, visited England for the purpose of buying a boat capable of making the twelve thousand-mile voyage back to his homeland. After looking around various boat-yards, he found what he wanted in the Mignonette, a yawl-rigged yacht with an overall length of fifty-two feet and weighing nineteen tons gross.

Now came the problem of hiring a crew to sail the vessel back for him. Mr Want finally secured the services of a Captain Dudley, promising him a fee of two hundred pounds to sail the yacht to Sydney. In turn, Captain Dudley selected the rest of his crew.

The Mignonette left Southampton on 19 May 1884. On board were Captain Dudley, two seamen – Stephens and Brooks – and a cabin boy, Richard Parker, aged seventeen. The vessel made good time, averaging over one hundred nautical miles a day, and crossed the line on 17 June.

But with her entry into southern latitudes, the weather changed. There were frequent storms and gales, and on

3 July the ship foundered and the crew had to abandon fast. They barely had time to launch the dinghy into the raging seas – damaging it in the process – and grabbed just two one-pound tins of vegetables. They had no drinking water. They were adrift hundreds of miles from the nearest land, being lashed by constant gales and unable to rest for a moment because they had to keep bailing out the dinghy. Some planks had been damaged in the launch, and they had to stuff clothing into the cracks.

After four days they were in a pitiful state, without rest, soaked to the skin and without food or water, they were in a state of complete physical exhaustion. They had been lucky enough to catch a turtle, but unwisely ate it too quickly, and consumed the contents of the two tins of vegetables in a single day. Eleven days after taking to the dinghy, they were without a scrap of food and had to depend on rain for drinking water.

Day followed dreadful day, the men becoming more weak and emaciated with each passing hour. On the sixteenth day the captain broke. He suggested that in order to save the lives of himself, Stephens and Brooks, the cabin boy should be killed and eaten.

Brooks was horrified by the suggestion and refused to have anything to do with the plan. But he was single. Captain Dudley and Stephens were married men with dependants. Parker, the cabin boy, was unaware of the discussion. He had given way to temptation and drank sea-water, with the result that he lay in a fit. His folly seemed an obvious excuse to Dudley and Stephens that he should die.

They agreed that if by the following morning no sail was sighted, or rain fell, they would butcher Parker and eat him. The next dawn saw no rain or sail, and so Dudley, after praying for the boy's forgiveness, quickly slit his throat. The boy was too weak to resist. He was then eaten. By a cruel irony, rain fell the very next day . . .

For four more days the boat bobbed on the ocean, a

tiny speck lost in the vastness. Finally, on 28 July, a sail was sighted and they were rescued by a German freighter, *Montezuma*, bound for Falmouth. Dudley, Stephens and Brooks were tenderly nursed back to health and finally landed back in England.

They had no need to admit killing Parker; any excuse would have served to explain the disappearance of the cabin boy. But they made a full and frank confession, and were arraigned for murder on the high seas. Magistrates found Brooks innocent, but Dudley and Stephens were sent for trial at the assizes.

On 6 November 1884, at the Devon and Cornwall Winter Assizes, before Baron Huddleston, both men appeared in the dock to be tried for the murder of Richard Parker. The case had aroused a good deal of public sympathy and a large sum had been subscribed by the public to pay for the defence. Mr Collins, QC, counsel for the defence, realised he faced an almost impossible task. All he could plead on behalf of his clients was justified murder; in short: *sheer necessity*.

'Was there ever,' he asked the jury, 'a case where necessity could be pleaded with greater justice? The necessity of these men was dire. There was no escape from death unless one died for the others. These men saw death staring them in the face. The only way to escape death was by the sacrificing of one. Surely the circumstances which have been stated show there was no escape except by the course these men in the dock pursued.'

It was a shocking defence in the light of Victorian morality. (Today, a defence counsel would probably plead temporary insanity.) Yet such was the effect of his speech on the jury that the judge feared they would return a Not Guilty verdict. Accordingly, he directed the jury to find the facts proved in a special verdict, and leave the issue of guilt itself to the court. The jury duly returned a verdict that the facts had been proved, and 'prayed the advice of the Court thereupon'. The case was then adjourned to the Royal Courts of Justice and was heard before five judges. The Crown was represented by the Attorney-General, and three silks. The defence was once more argued by Mr Collins.

Again Mr Collins advanced the point that necessity excused an act which would otherwise be a crime, and gave the illustration of two drowning men on a plank which would only support one. If one thrust the other off, was the survivor a murderer?

The Attorney-General was outraged. 'My learned friend has pleaded the necessity of hunger and thirst for this murder. The law of England says that if a man is dying of hunger he must not steal food. How, then, can these men be held guiltless of murder? If you hold that the killing of the boy was justified, you must also hold that a man may not only take food from a living person, but might kill that person to obtain food.'

In delivering judgement, the Lord Chief Justice stated the law clearly. He then went on to say: 'The real question in the case is whether killing under the circumstances set forth is or is not murder. The contention that it could be anything else was, to the minds of us all, both new and strange.' He described the defence as ' . . . dangerous, immoral, and opposed to all legal principles. To preserve one's life is, generally speaking, a duty; but it may be the plainest duty, the highest duty, to sacrifice it.'

Without donning the black cap, the Lord Chief Justice then formally sentenced both men to death. Later, it was announced that a respite had been granted by Her Majesty, and on 13 December the sentences upon both men were commuted to six month's imprisonment without hard labour.

It was a remarkable conclusion. Victorian morality was much stronger than our own, yet in this case the law appeared to act extremely leniently towards this 'new and strange . . . dangerous and immoral' defence. It would appear to modern observers that there could be no defence for this crime.

5

SURVIVAL IN THE ANDES

We turn now to a modern case which illustrates an age-old truth: in life-threatening situations human beings lose all their inhibitions and acquire cultural values. We become what we were designed to be: animals. And there is no shame in that.

At about half past three in the afternoon of Friday, 13 October 1972, a Fairchild F-227 of the Uruguayan Air Force carrying an amateur rugby team crashed among the peaks of the snow-covered Andes Mountains, while ferrying the team from Argentina to play a match in Chile. The aircraft actually came down in Argentina, although it was extremely close to the border with Chile.

The plane was flown by two air force pilots of great experience, but a severe pocket of air turbulence had forced the plane down. As well as the rugby team, the plane was carrying passengers anxious to visit relatives in Chile.

Of the forty-five passengers and crew, many died on impact. The aircraft lost both wings and its tail section. Two boys were sucked out of the rear section as the fuselage hit the ground and slid along the deep snow like a sledge before finally coming to rest. The plane had been miles off course, and the survivors were stranded in a mountain range which averaged 13,000 feet in height, with peaks as high as 20,000 feet, and one, Aconcagua, being the highest mountain in the Western Hemisphere, only 6,000 feet short of Mount Everest at 22,834 feet.

Nothing grows at this altitude, and any rocks free from

snow are barren lumps of granite in a terrain composed of fifty-foot-deep snow for the most part. The bitterly cold wind, which quickly robs the body of heat, and the lack of food, were an ever-present threat to the lives of those who had survived the crash.

The young men of the rugby team were known as the Old Christians, alumni of the Stella Maris College in Montevideo, a Catholic school run and staffed by five Irish lay brothers. The boys were thus devout Catholics and had been educated in discipline and self-control. Now that training was to pay off.

The captain of the team, Marcello Perez, organized the rescue of those survivors who had been trapped in the fuselage and were screaming in agony with broken legs and suchlike. Many of the injuries had been caused by the seats crashing into one another in a concertina fashion on impact. Two medical students, Canessa and Zerbino, practised their first-aid on the casualties.

Most of the adults had been killed, including a husband and wife, and the pilot. The co-pilot was still alive but had smashed into the instrument panel and could not be freed. He was in agony and obviously dying, and asked the boys to fetch him his revolver so that he could shoot himself. They refused. As Catholics, they regarded suicide as a mortal sin. The co-pilot died soon afterwards. Of the original forty-five in the plane, thirty-two had survived the crash. In the days and weeks which followed, many others were to die in turn.

The immediate situation was grim. There was no food or medicine, and little could be done to aid the badly injured. As each one died, his or her body was dragged outside the fuselage and buried in the snow. The fuselage – what remained of the plane – was now home to the survivors. It was resting at 11,500 feet near an extinct volcano, and because its roof was painted white, it would not be seen by rescue planes against the surrounding snow.

The survivors huddled in the fuselage and rationed out

precious squares of chocolate, eating snow for moisture. But they were fighting a losing battle against the harsh reality of nature. They were lost in the most hostile of terrains, and the aircraft radio was dead. One by one they died and were tossed outside in the days which followed.

On the fourth day after the crash, four boys set out to walk to the rear section of the plane, a couple of miles away. They came aross the two bodies which had been sucked out of the plane, and in the tail section found a little food.

By now, aircraft from Chile, Argentina and Uruguay were involved in the search for the missing plane, but after a couple of fruitless weeks the search was abandoned as futile. However, the parents of those lost in the plane hired private pilots to continue the search, and even enlisted the help of the Dutch clairvoyant, Gerard Croiset. All these efforts proved to be in vain.

By the ninth day the remaining survivors were in a bad way, extremely weak from lack of food and becoming desperate. Now the idea of having to eat the flesh of their dead companions had surfaced and was being seriously debated. Canessa, the medical student, argued that they needed protein if they were to survive, and the only source of protein available to them lay in the flesh of the dead: in the bodies lying outside, conveniently refrigerated by the snow. He explained that if they did not eat soon, they would lack the strength even to cut meat from the bodies.

The idea was met with revulsion, but Canessa gave the debate a moral dimension, pointing out that they had a duty to stay alive by any means at their disposal. If they did not think of the corpses as human beings, but simply as meat, it would be easier.

By the end of two weeks the boys were hungry enough – and desperate enough – to cut flesh from the bodies and put it on the roof of the plane to 'cure'. Canessa, took the lead, first praying to God, and then putting the strip of flesh into his mouth and swallowing. Other boys followed his example – but not all. Some refused to eat human flesh, so powerful was the taboo instilled in them.

The cutting of strips of flesh from the bodies became an industry, with some boys even stealing strips of the flesh destined for the communal pot. There were now twenty-seven survivors. Some of the boys had begun cooking the flesh on aluminium sheets over a fire, but Canessa discouraged this practice, on the grounds that meat loses much of its nutritive value in the process of cooking. For maximum value, the meat had to be eaten raw . . .

The boys who refused to eat the flesh from religious scruples became very emaciated, and their companions pleaded with them to eat, one saying to them: 'Think of it as Communion. Think of it as the body and blood of Christ, because this is food that God has given us because He wants us to live.' But still they would not eat, and duly died.

During the night following the seventeenth day, an avalanche of snow killed eight of the survivors, burying and suffocating them.

The eighteen who remained were now at their lowest ebb, suffering alternately from diarrhoea or constipation. It was decided that the fittest among them should try and walk out to Chile to seek help and rescue for the rest. Another boy died before this could take place.

On the morning of Friday, 17 November – after a month in the mountains – three young men set out to fetch help. They were Roberto Canessa, Antonio Vizintin and Nado Parrado. They reached the tail section of the plane that day, found some food, and slept there overnight. Next morning they set off again, wearing rugby boots and extra layers of clothing, and carrying supplies of meat in their pockets. That night they slept in the snow, and realizing the futility of walking deeper into the mountains, returned in despair to the plane. In their absence another of the survivors had died.

Canessa was a tower of strength to the others. He organized parties to dig up the bodies from the snow and removed the brains to eat, saying they contained valuable minerals. On 10 December another survivor died. Parrado told his companions that if rations ran low, they had his permission to eat his mother and sister, who had died in the crash.

On 12 December, Parrado, Vizintin and Canessa again set out on a trek to seek rescue, climbing peak after peak, each revealing yet another peak to climb. Vizintin was sent back to the plane so that the other two could share his rations and carry on a little longer.

By Saturday, 16 December, Parrado and Canessa had reached the top of yet another peak and were making the descent on the other side. They suddenly glimpsed a fertile valley, with a cow in a meadow, and realized that they could not be far from civilization.

By the tenth day both boys were exhausted and near to collapse when they spotted a peasant on the other side of a river, sitting by a fire. They called out to him to throw across a pen and paper. On this Parrado wrote: 'I come from a plane that fell in the mountains.' The peasant – a Chilean – threw some food across to them before departing. Three hours later a man arrived with a horse to carry them to the nearest village. They reached it on Thursday, 21 December – seventy days after the plane had crashed in the Andes, and after walking for ten days through the mountains. It was truly a heroic feat of endurance.

It seemed incredible to the authorities that anyone could have survived for so long in the mountains, but helicopters were sent off to fetch the survivors. Parrado sat in one machine to guide the rescue party, and the ragged survivors were taken to the Central Hospital in Santiago.

Medical examinations revealed that all the survivors had suffered drastic weight loss and had serious deficiencies of vitamins, fats and proteins. The press were hounding them for interviews, and the survivors now realized that the awful truth must come out. They had already told doctors what they had done, and had received absolution from a priest.

'The Miracle of the Andes', as the press were calling it, had only been made possible by the decision to eat human flesh, and the sixteen survivors had to live with the consequences.

On 26 December a Santiago newspaper published a photograph of a half-eaten human leg lying in the snow by the crashed aircraft, and the truth was out. The survivors held a press conference at which they defended their action in the name of their religion. The Archbishop of Montevideo said: 'Morally, I see no objection, since it was a question of survival. It is always necessary to eat whatever is to hand, in spite of the repugnance it might evoke.'

The quibble came about those who had refused to eat human flesh and had consequently died. Had they committed suicide – a mortal sin – by their refusal to survive? The question remained unanswered.

On 18 January 1973, members of the Uruguayan Air Force flew to the wreckage of the plane in the Andes and collected the human remains from around the plane, giving them a decent burial. A large stone cross was erected over the grave, and then the aircraft which had been home to the sixteen survivors was doused in petrol and burned, as if to purify the mountains and remove all trace of that terrible secret which had stained the virgin snow . . .

6
A CRASH DIET

A very similar case to the Andes survivors' was that of bush-pilot Marten Hartwell, who crashed in his light aircraft in a remote part of the vast Canadian forest in midwinter, near to the Arctic Circle and with temperatures constantly at -30 degrees Centigrade.

His private plane was carrying a pregnant Eskimo woman, a nurse, and a fourteen-year-old Eskimo boy suffering from acute appendicitis. Hartwell broke both legs in the crash, and shattered a kneecap.

The German-born pilot had taken off from Cambridge Bay on 8 November 1972, heading for a hospital in Yellowknife. But unable to get a satisfactory compass or radio bearing, he came down too low and crashed into a hillside.

The nurse died instantly from a fractured skull; the Eskimo woman a few hours later from a broken neck. The boy was uninjured, and under the pilot's instruction he constructed an emergency tent and set up rabbit traps. They caught no game, and lived on a small supply of corned beef and sugar. On the twentieth day there was nothing left. On 30 November, Hartwell noted in a diary he was keeping: *Still alive. David is going to die tomorrow and I two or three days later. No food. My legs don't carry me.*

On 2 December, Hartwell dragged himself to the nearest tree and hacked off branches to make a small fire, in an attempt to make soup from the lichen on the branches. It was useless. 'There was no way out but to eat human flesh, and this is what I did,' he said.

Hartwell told his story in the TV programme 'Survive', on Channel 4. He explained: 'I asked the boy if he would eat human flesh, since it was the only thing we had around. He said: "Shut up, I am going to die now."' Hartwell added: 'David had determined to die, and died quite soon after this decision.'

Hartwell went on: 'The worst thing was to take the first bite. The horror of what I was doing didn't bother me after that.' But he admitted that he was consciously worried about the attitude of society towards him, and even thought they might hang him for what he was doing. It was during this period that he lost his faith in God. Until his rescue on 9 December, he sustained himself on the flesh of the twenty-seven-year-old nurse. He had survived for an incredible thirty-two days.

He said that if faced with a similar situation in the future, 'I would say: Shut up I am going to die now – like David did.'

Perhaps it is a natural reaction to start looking at dead people as food sources in dire straits. Certainly in the last war the Russians resorted to eating the bodies of the dead during the siege of Leningrad, having first consumed every dog, cat and rat in the city.

A much more detailed record of cannibalism was given by Lord Russell of Liverpool in his book, *The Scourge of the Swastika*. Writing of Belsen, Russell said:

During the last few months of the camp's existence the short-age of food was so acute that the prisoners resorted to canni-balism, and one former British internee gave evidence at the trial of the Commandant and some of his staff that when engaged in clearing away dead bodies, as many as one in ten had a piece cut from the thigh or other part of the body, which had been taken and eaten, and that he had seen many people in the act of doing this. To such lengths had they been brought by the pangs of hunger.

The witness said: 'I noticed on many occasions a very strange wound at the back of the thigh on many of the dead. First of all I dismissed it as a gunshot wound at close quarters, but after seeing a few more I asked a friend and he told me that many of the prisoners were cutting chunks out of the bodies to eat. On my very next visit to the mortuary I actually saw a prisoner whip out a knife, cut a portion out of the leg of a dead body and put it quickly into his mouth, naturally frightened of being seen in the act of doing so. I leave it to your imagination to realize to what state the prisoners were reduced, for men to risk eating bits of flesh cut from corpses.'

What we have learned from all this, of course, is that there is no *natural* aversion to eating human flesh. It is an acquired cultural taboo which disappears surprisingly quickly in the face of famine or acute hunger.

A common expression to describe the competitive nature of modern society is to say 'It's a dog-eat-dog world.' That is a euphemism to hide an ugly truth which we would rather not face. Dogs *do* eat dogs, of course, but what we really mean is that it is a man-eat-man world out there. And of men eating men we have records in plenty.

This is also the basis of all those cannibal jokes about the missionary in the cooking-pot. We laugh at what we fear most: the dark, hidden side of our natures which is only exposed when an awful calamity overtakes us. Then we reveal the fangs behind the smile . . .

PART III: CANNIBALISM FOR PROFIT

1

SAWNEY BEAN

Traditional Tales of the Lowlands by John Nicholson of Kircudbright is the authority for and record of the atrocities committed by Sawney Bean, a bandit who lived during the reign of James I of Scotland. He is generally referred to as being legendary, but the writings about him are so detailed that it is impossible not to think that he actually existed.

Born sometime in the late fourteenth century, Bean was brought up in East Lothian and lived out in the country some eight or nine miles from Edinburgh. At first he followed his father's trade of hedger and ditcher, but found working for a living to be tiresome.

He took up quite early in life with a woman 'as viciously inclined as himself', and together they set up home in a cave in Galloway, close to the sea. They were to live in that cave for some twenty-five years, never venturing into nearby towns or villages, and produced many children.

By a process of incest the family grew into a gang of some forty-six individuals, consisting of eight sons, six daughters, eighteen grandsons and fourteen grand-daughters. They lived on the proceeds of highway robbery, killing the occasional traveller and eating his body. Surplus flesh was pickled in brine for lean times. There can be little doubt that Bean ate human flesh not from any particular taste for it, but simply because it was free. His murders were strictly for economic reasons.

Although no one survived an attack to warn of the

Beans' existence, the high disappearance rate of travellers in the area was noted. And the family grew careless, so glutted with flesh that they began to throw unwanted arms and legs into the sea. When these were washed up on to the shores, it caused 'astonishment and terror', as the book tells us.

Locals began speculating about the number of people who had gone missing over the years. The Bean family always used to attack in strength, ambushing a party of travellers – never more than six in number – and quickly killing them. While they butchered the victims for their meat, they no doubt also used their cash to buy bread and vegetables. A diet of meat alone could never have sufficed for twenty-five years.

The authorities, aware that there was a predator in the area, adopted the usual tactic of executing people at random in the hope that they had got the right man. They tended to execute the innkeeper with whom the missing people had last lodged. This had the effect in time of depopulating the area.

The capture of the Bean family came quite by accident. They attacked a man and his wife returning home from a fair, cut the throat of the woman, 'and fell to sucking her blood with great gusto . . . when this had been done, they ripped up her belly and pulled out all her entrails.'

While the husband, mounted on a horse, fought for his life, another party of travellers came along and drove the Bean family off, saving the husband's life. He rode to Glasgow to raise the alarm.

He told Glasgow magistrates of his encounter with the murderous family, whose existence had gone unsuspected for a quarter of a century.

News of the affair reached the ear of the King, and he set out himself to hunt down the family, taking with him four hundred men and a pack of bloodhounds.

It was the bloodhounds who located the family cave; the hunters would have passed by without noticing it, but the smell of meat was too strong for the dogs to ignore. The hunters now invaded the cave in strength and found an astonishing scene.

Human flesh was found hanging up to cure, and various parts of human bodies were being smoked over fires. The Bean family watched the hunters with apathetic eyes, making no attempt to defend their territory. They were all captured alive and were taken in chains to Edinburgh, where they were committed to the Tollbooth, and from there they were taken on to Leith.

Judgement was swift. They were all 'executed without any process' – meaning without the formality of a trial. So great was the horror that their crimes aroused in the populace and the King that their punishment was even more barbaric. They were executed very slowly, the men bleeding to death after their hands and legs had been chopped off, while the women – who had been forced to watch this – were afterwards burned alive in three great fires. The book tells us: 'They all in general died without the least sign of repentance, but continued cursing . . . to the very last gasp of life.'

The forces of law and order, of government and leadership, have always proved to be far more terrible and barbaric than any common criminal who threatens their existence.

2
PACKER: THE MAN WHO ATE THE DEMOCRATS

The story begins in the bitter winter of 1873, when Alfred G. Packer, a Union Army veteran, led a party of gold-prospectors into the Rocky Mountains in Colorado, USA. The party became stranded – and Packer was the only survivor. He had kept himself alive by eating the flesh of his dead companions. The question was: did they die from natural causes, or did Packer kill them to eat them?

Packer was described as a prospector who knew Colorado as well as any man living, and a man who had a nose for gold. It was for these reasons that the party hired Packer to act as their guide.

In the autumn of 1873 Packer, then in his mid-twenties, led the team of nineteen prospectors from Salt Lake City, Utah, to the San Juan country, loaded down with supplies and equipment. The weeks passed and the weary men saw nothing but barren country, eventually arriving close to the snow-capped peaks.

On the point of starvation, they stumbled across an Indian camp, expecting to be butchered. To their surprise the Indians treated them with great hospitality and fed and looked after them. Learning of their hazardous proposed expedition, the Indian leader, Chief Ouray, succeeded in persuading ten of the party to abandon the futile quest, and they returned to Salt Lake City, sadder and wiser men.

The rest promised to pay Packer well to continue as their guide, and so they remained at the Indian camp until they were fully recovered, still determined to hunt for gold. All the Indians could do was to supply them with provisions and advise them to follow the course of the Gunnison River.

Alfred Packer was now the undisputed leader of the expedition. Boasting of his knowledge of the area, he lured his companions on by telling them that rich seams of gold had recently been discovered near the source of the Rio Grande River. He claimed to be able to guide the party to the area by a much shorter route. However, four of the party insisted on following the Gunnison River, as recommended by the Indians, and Packer led the remaining five men, Israel Swan, Frank Miller, George Noon, Shannon Bell and a man named Humphrey, on his own route.

Of the four men who followed the Gunnison River, two died of starvation before reaching the Los Pinos Agency in February 1874. General Adams was in command of the agency, and saw to it that the two men were treated before beginning their trek back to civilization.

In March 1874, General Adams was absent from the agency on business in Denver when a wild-looking man appeared at the agency, begging for food. His face was hideously bloated, but he was in surprisingly good physical condition, everything considered. He gave his name as Packer and explained that his five companions had deserted him while he was ill, leaving him with only a rifle to shoot wild game to survive. He still carried that rifle.

After a ten-day stay at the agency, Packer left, saying that he intended making his way to his brother's home in Pennsylvania. Along the way he stopped in many bars, drinking heavily, and appeared to be in possession of a considerable quantity of money. The conflicting stories he told in those bars about the fate of his companions led to speculation that he had in fact murdered them.

Word of all this reached General Adams, who decided to have Packer tracked down and arrested. He arranged a meeting between Packer and those men who had abandoned the expedition, and it immediately became apparent that most of Packer's story was untrue. General Adams had Packer tightly fettered and taken back to the agency, where he was kept in solitary confinement.

On 2 April 1874, two Indians arrived at the agency, holding what they claimed were strips of 'white man's meat'. They had found it just outside the agency, where the snow had kept it well preserved. It was in fact human flesh, which Packer must have been carrying, and then dumped when he reached safety.

When Packer was shown the flesh he gave a loud groan of despair and fell to the ground. He then made the following statement:

When I and five others left Ouray's camp, we estimated that we had sufficient provisions for the long and arduous journey before us, but our food rapidly disappeared and we were soon on the verge of starvation. We dug roots from the ground upon which we subsisted for some days, but as they were not nutritious and as the extreme cold had driven all animals and birds to shelter, the situation became desperate. Strange looks came into the eyes of each of the party and they all became suspicious of each other. One day I went out to gather wood for the fire and when I returned I found that Mr Swan, the oldest man in the party, had been struck on the head and killed, and the remainder of the party were in the act of cutting up the body preparatory to eating it. His money, amounting to $2,000, was divided among the remainder of the party.

This food only lasted a few days and I suggested that Miller be the next victim, because of the large amount of flesh he carried. His skull was split open with a hatchet as he was in the act of picking up a piece of wood. Humphrey and Noon were the next victims. Bell and I then entered into a solemn compact that as we were the only ones left, we would stand by each other whatever befell, and rather than harm each other we would die of starvation.

One day Bell said: 'I can stand it no longer!' and he rushed at me like a famished tiger, at the same time attempting to strike me with his gun. I parried the blow and killed him with a hatchet. I then cut his flesh into strips which I carried with me as I pursued my journey. When I espied the agency from the top of the hill, I threw away the strips I had left, and I confess I did so reluctantly as I had grown fond of human flesh, especially that portion around the breast.

One thing is certain: Parker never wrote or dictated this statement. The wording is not that of an ignorant prospector, but rather that of a military man.

Packer agreed to guide a party to where he had left the murdered men, but during the night, while sleeping out in the open, he assaulted his guard with intent to murder him and escape, but was overpowered. He was taken back to the agency in fetters and was there handed over to the sheriff.

In June 1874, an artist named Reynolds was out sketching in the wilderness when he came across the bodies of five men. Four of them were lying in a row, and the fifth, minus its head, was lying a short distance away. The bodies of Bell, Swan, Humphrey and Noon had rifle bullet wounds in the back of the skull, and when Miller's head was found, it had been crushed by a blow from a rifle butt.

The find made a complete nonsense of Packer's statement. A path led from the bodies to a nearby hut, where blankets and possessions belonging to the murdered men were found, and it was apparent that Packer had lived in that cabin for many days, making frequent trips to the bodies for his supply of meat. Each body had its breast cut away to the ribs. The sheriff now obtained a warrant charging Parker with five murders, but in the meantime he escaped.

On 29 January 1883 – some nine years later – General Adams received a letter posted from Cheyenne, Wyoming, in which a Salt Lake City prospector said he had met Packer face to face in that area, going under the name of John Schwartze. It was believed that he was a member of a gang of outlaws.

General Adams alerted the lawmen in Cheyenne, and on 12 March 1883 Sheriff Sharpless of Laramie County arrested Packer and brought him to Lake City, Colorado, to stand trial.

Packer's trial began on 3 April 1883, when he was charged with the murder of Israel Swan in Hinsdale County on 1 March 1874. The prosecution proved that each of the murdered men had been in possession of considerable sums of money, none of which was found on the mutilated bodies. It was a clear case of murder for gain.

Packer, in his defence, claimed that he had only killed Bell, and then in self-defence. He told a story of his companions fighting among themselves and of Bell firing at him. This completely contradicted what he had said in his original statement, and the jury did not believe his new account. On 13 April the jury found Packer guilty of murder, and voted for the death penalty. Packer appealed to the Supreme Court and was granted a stay of execution. Meanwhile, he was being lodged in Gunnison Jail to save him from a lynch mob.

In October 1885 the Supreme Court granted him a new trial, and the prosecution decided this time to try him on five charges of manslaughter. Packer was found guilty of each charge and was sentenced to serve eight years for each offence, making a total of forty years.

Sentencing Packer, Judge Melville Gerry said: 'There were only seven Democrats in Hinsdale County, and you ate five of them, you depraved Republican son of a bitch!' It must have been the most unintentionally comic line ever uttered by a judge at any trial.

Packer served seventeen years at hard labour before being released. He proclaimed his innocence throughout all those years. He died on a ranch near Denver on 24 April 1907, aged sixty-five, having been pardoned on 1 January 1901.

Packer had become famous in those years. A song, 'The Man Who Ate Democrats', became very popular, and students at Colorado State University named their dining room after him.

Packer, an unlikely folk-hero, was described as 'a tall man with long dark curling hair, dark moustache and goatee, with deep-set grey eyes'. Gradually, over the years, the suspicion began to grow that Packer was innocent after all.

The evidence was re-examined. He had rejected the advice of an Indian chief and pushed on through heavy snows, staggering back some weeks later with his story of the hunger-crazed Bell having killed and cannibalized the others, while he shot Shannon Wilson Bell in self-defence, finishing him off with a hatchet.

Packer had admitted having survived the winter by feasting off the flesh of his companions – but claimed they were already dead, having been murdered by Bell.

The evidence against Packer was that he had seemed too *fit*, the Indian Chief Ouray who saw him commented: 'You too damn fat!' And he was found in possession of money, a gun, and a knife belonging to the murdered men. Could he really have been innocent, guilty of nothing more than having feasted off already dead men?

What brought this old case back into the news was an announcement in July 1989 that a team of scientists were to search Dead Man's Gulch, scene of the murders, in the hope of locating the remains of the victims. The team planned to use sophisticated radar for this purpose. The leader of the scientific expedition, Professor James Starrs, said that he planned to examine the skeletons to see if all the men had died from bullets fired from the same gun.

If they had, then Packer's memory would stand condemned. But if one of the bodies bore bullets from a different gun, then it might be that Packer had been telling the truth after all: that his companions had started fighting among themselves.

The results are now in, the one hundred and fifteen-year-old mystery solved. A jury of thirteen experts who dug up the skeletons agreed with the original jury verdict, saying that 'Packer was guilty as sin.'

James Starrs, a professor of law and forensic science at Washington State University, said the bones proved 'beyond a shadow of a doubt' that Packer killed all five men.

'It is as plain as a pikestaff that Packer was the one who was on the attack, not Bell,' said Professor Starrs. Wounds on the bones of three of the victims 'were caused with a hatchet-like instrument at a time when these persons were defending themselves from the attack of an aggressor,' he said. The marks suggested that the victims had raised their arms to ward off the blows.

Professor Starrs and his team of experts on archaeology, anthropology, pathology and firearms said that the angle of blade marks on the bones from which the flesh had been taken, including the bones believed to be Bell's, indicated that the cuts were all made by the same person, a clear sign that Packer's story was false.

The Professor said that Packer 'was having his flesh fillets morning noon and night' even though he could have lived by killing rabbits. The professor described Packer as having been 'base, brutish and barbaric'.

The new and conclusive discoveries will do nothing to damage Packer's reputation. He will still be celebrated in legend and song. But the whole story is a grim testimony to just how wild the Wild West really was . . .

3

LUETGERT THE SAUSAGE-MAKER

The American version of the Sweeney Todd legend happened to be true . . . In 1897 Adloph L. Luetgert, a sausage manufacturer of Chicago, Illinois, murdered his second wife, Louisa, and dumped her body in a vat he used for boiling sausage meat. To this day many Chicagoans refer to Luetgert as the man who turned his wife into sausages, and children at play in that city still chant: 'Adolf was a dirty rat/Who boiled his wife for sausage fat . . . '

Adloph Luetgert was born in Germany in 1849 and emigrated to America in the 1870s with the ambition of becoming the best sausage-maker in America. Within three years he had become one of the leading butchers in Chicago, and his sausages were famous throughout the state – particularly among the large German population, as well as the Dutch, Poles and others who liked well-seasoned and flavoured sausages.

But Luetgert was like a publican who enjoys too much of that which he sells. He had a prodigious appetite and came to weigh some two hundred and fifty pounds. He was a coarse bully of a man who had a sexual appetite to match. He spent many nights away from home in the company of his mistresses, even installing one of them at his factory as a 'secretary'.

As a consequence of his activities, his marriage and business suffered. His second wife, Louisa, complained that he neglected her, and salesmen and other business callers complained that they could never find him at his office. His marriage was foundering, and his factory was slowly going bankrupt.

When Louisa nagged him to put more money into the business, he flew into a furious rage and attempted to throttle her. When she escaped from his deadly embrace and fled from the house, he chased her down the street, waving a revolver and shouting lurid threats.

Meanwhile, he was grumbling to his mistresses about his wife. 'She annoys me! I could take her and crush her!' he said to one; and to another: 'She is as cold as a dead fish . . . Sex with her is like trying to flog a dead horse.' And if anyone should know about a dead horse, it was a butcher.

Louisa was in the habit of spending time with her mother now and again, and Luetgert was only too glad of her visits to his mother-in-law, whom he hated. With his wife out of the way, he could even bring his mistresses into the marriage bed.

In early May 1897, Louisa vanished. A few days later her mother turned up at the factory demanding to know where her daughter was. 'I thought she was staying with you!' Luetgert said. 'No,' the mother replied, 'she has not visited me at all. I think we should report her missing to the police.'

In vain, Luetgert protested that as a prominent businessman he could not afford the scandal of having the police pry into his personal affairs. After a few days, the mother did go to the police, and Luetgert was questioned, while detectives made inquiries.

A witness was found who had seen Louisa Luetgert on the night of 1 May following her husband up an alley behind the factory. That was the last time she was ever seen alive. And that same night Luetgert had sent his night-watchman out on a series of unnecessary errands, while he worked alone among his steaming vats. The following morning one of the employees noticed that one of the vats contained a strange brown slime, as well as obvious slivers of bone. When the man, named Frank

Odorowsky, pointed this out to Luetgert, he was told to keep quiet and promised a job for life.

None of this information augured well for either Luetgert or his missing wife. His whole attitude was suspicious. He refused to hire a private detective to search for his missing wife. He suggested she might have gone back to Germany. He appeared unconcerned, still drinking vast quantities of strong German beer and dallying with the ladies.

The police decided to search the factory from top to bottom, and they were particularly interested in the vats. All were emptied of their contents and searched. Three revealed nothing, but the fourth vat had a very interesting sludge at its bottom, which proved to contain, among other things, two gold wedding rings – one of which was engraved with the initials *LL* – a metal corset clip, human bone fragments and human teeth.

Faced with this evidence, Luetgert blustered. The rings were not those of his wife. She had swollen fingers from arthritis and would never have been able to take the rings off – but her mother identified them as having been the property of her daughter. The bone fragments had come from an animal, as had the teeth, and were in fact the remains of pigs used in the manufacture of sausages. If the teeth were human, he said, they could have been the false teeth of an employee which had fallen accidentally into the vat.

When taken into custody for the murder of his wife, Luetgert continued to bluster. The rings had not belonged to his wife – he should know, he was her husband. So the mother had identified them? She was seventy and blind as a bat. What if the rings bore the initials *LL*? There must be thousands of women with those initials . . .

But the police pathologist had been busy with those bone fragments and the teeth. Louisa Luetgert's dentist, Herr Hans Kaufman, checked the teeth against the records of his patient and positively identified them as being teeth he had supplied to the missing woman as part of a dental plate in 1892. The pathologist had identified those bone fragments as being of human origin. And it was true that Louisa Luetgert would never have been able to slip those rings over her swollen knuckles.

There was only one conclusion. The entire body of the missing wife had been melted in Vat No. 4 at the meat plant by Luetgert, who had made her part of his sausage production line. Just how he had killed his wife remained a mystery, although there were always plenty of sharp knives in a meat plant; and just how he had lured his wife into the factory was unknown, but it would have been easy to find a pretext.

The trial of Luetgert for murdering his wife proved to be a sensation, with huge crowds lining the pavement to gain admittance to the court, to listen to a succession of Luetgert's mistresses testify against him. The tabloid press had a field day. But they never bothered to get the reaction of Luetgert's former customers: the people who had eaten his sausages – and possibly most of the evidence.

Luetgert had two trials – the first was declared a mistrial – and he was subsequently convicted of murder in the first degree, being sentenced to serve a life sentence in Joliet Prison. He continued to protest his innocence for a long time afterwards. He died in his cell on 27 July 1899 from a heart attack, having spent fourteen years without a woman. But he had made a confession of sorts to his crime, saying he had been 'possessed by the devil' when he killed his wife.

The sale of sausages was boycotted for many years afterwards in Illinois, and even in neighbouring Michigan, by a population nauseated by the evidence in the case. Never again could they feel sure of what – or who – they were eating.

4

THREE GERMAN CANNIBALS

Examples to prove the maxim that crimes should be viewed in the context of their time came in the grisly and sordid cases of Grossmann, Haarmaan and Denke. All three men were either cannibals or turned their fellow citizens into unwitting cannibals, and their activities came suddenly to the public consciousness, being roughly contemporary.

All three cases happened in Germany after the First World War, and the context was that of a nation which was economically and spiritually bankrupt. The old order had come tumbling down; conventional morality had gone by the board, and an entire nation was caught up in a frantic spiral of rising prices and increasing shortages.

It was the time of the spiv and the black market. People queued ten-deep for bread, and meat was an almost unobtainable luxury. The honest and hard-working citizen was condemned to perish in a Sadean nightmare world where virtue was punished and vice rewarded. Only by resorting to the extensive system of black market – the *Schieber Markt*, or thieves' market – could the bare necessities of life be obtained.

The people had been uprooted, displaced. Many of the shifting population became tramps, and a wave of lawlessness swept over Germany. There was talk of revolution. The communists were active, and the police force, badly understaffed and underpaid, spent most of its time spying on the various rival political factions, making use of paid informers by the thousand. The police also became notorious for their propensity to accept bribes – even from the most vicious of criminals.

William Bolitho, in his classic *Murder For Profit*, examined the Haarmaan case at length, prefacing it with a lengthy introduction which was almost Marxist in its condemnation of the State.

> What that our mass-murderers have done that the State cannot outmatch? . . . Any first-class State in the world could show as many killings every year, done on its own profession, not from hate or impulse, but from its cold and calculated self-interest . . . Where could a nation so miserable be found that it would not gladly use a thousand lives for a handker-chief of territory? . . . in the neighbourhood of a war, such as the last in which 12,000,000 perished, the mass-murderer loses all claim to the wholesale and becomes an infinitesimal wretch, engaged in minute wickedness unworthy of attention . . .

Bolitho was writing in 1926, when the Great War was a recent memory whose glory had faded and its generals were coming to be regarded as inept butchers. But to equate the actions of the State with that of the individual is just a little too fanciful – even hysterical.

But in this time of social turmoil, creatures like Grossmann, Haarmaan and Denke flourished like maggots. It happened then – it can happen again.

5

GEORG KARL GROSSMANN

Grossmann, born in Neuruppin in 1863, kept himself alive during the period 1914 to 1921 by eating the flesh of the victims he lured to his room in Berlin. All his victims were female, and while the full tally will never be known, it may well have exceeded Haarmaan's fifty.

We have one account of the Grossmann case from the distinguished Swedish criminologist Söderman, a former head of the International Police Commission. Unfortunately, it is not a very trustworthy account, showing how even the serious academics can perpetuate myths. Söderman wrote:

In the early twenties there was a hot-dog vendor plying his trade at one of the railway stations in Berlin. His name was Grossmann and he had once been a butcher. Grossmann was about fifty years old; a thin, insignificant little man with a haggard face and a sloping moustache. About twice a month he used to spend a day on the platform where long-distance trains stopped. If he saw getting out of one of these carriages a girl who looked as if she was coming to the city to hunt for a job, he would approach her (provided she was fat enough) politely lift his cap and inquire whether he could be of any assistance. During the conversation he would drop a remark that he was in need of a housekeeper for his bachelor household and that she could have the job if she wanted.

Grossmann kept each of these girls for a couple of days, then murdered her. He cut up the bodies with a butcher's skill, kept the flesh and disposed of the balance in some sewer. Then he pickled the meat, ground it and put it into his sausages, which he later sold at the railway station. The constant stream of girls into his flat finally alerted some neighbours, who put the police on his track. Bundles of female clothes were discovered in the closets, and Grossmann finally confessed.

The truth was somewhat different. Grossmann was not a thin, insignificant little man, and he was never a hot-dog vendor. True, Grossmann's flat in Berlin was near the Silesian railway terminus, where he may have picked up his victims: homeless women looking for work and a place to stay. He had rented the flat the year before the war and kept it ever since. He had insisted on having a separate entrance to his quarters, and to the exclusive use of the kitchen – he never allowed the landlord to enter.

A big, surly man, he lived a mainly solitary existence, begging in the streets. His neighbours were surprised that he had not been called up for military service. The reason was his extensive criminal record. He had many convictions for sexual acts of a sadistic nature, including bestiality, and most of his offences had been against children. There can be little doubt that from an early age he was a degenerate of the worst type.

Grossmann never lacked female company, and rarely spent a night alone in his bed. But he killed many of his sleeping partners simply to sell their flesh for meat.

He was caught in August 1921, when Grossmann's landlord, who lived in the top-floor flat of the block, heard the noise of a struggle from Grossman's kitchen and called the police. They broke in and found on Grossmann's camp bed the trussed-up carcass of a recently killed girl, tied as if ready for butchering.

A search of the flat revealed evidence which indicated that Grossmann had killed and dismembered three women in his kitchen in the preceding three weeks.

Grossmann had listed the names of his victims in his diary. He laughed when he heard the death sentence pronounced upon him, and afterwards had fits of mania. He hanged himself in his cell with his braces, sparing the judicial system the final embarrassment of having to decapitate him.

6
FRITZ HAARMAAN

Haarmaan became known as the 'butcher of Hanover' when it was revealed that this homosexual killer had murdered around fifty young men between 1918 and his capture in 1924, and sold their bodies for meat after sodomizing them. He claimed to have killed his victims by biting through their windpipes. This may have been an exaggeration fuelled by a sadistic fantasy. But he did have a strong commercial instinct: he sold his victim's clothing on the black market.

Haarmaan was born in Hanover on 25 October 1879, the sixth child of an ill-assorted couple. The father, a locomotive stoker, was known as 'Sulky Olle' and his invalid wife was seven years his senior. She had become bedridden after the birth of Fritz. The couple simply did not get on, and they argued most over the children. Fritz became his mother's pet and grew to detest his father. From an early age Fritz took to playing with dolls and dressing as a girl.

At sixteen he was sent to a military school for NCOs, but was released when he began having epileptic fits. His father gave him a job in his small cigar factory, but the youth was lazy and often took days off.

On his days off he indecently assaulted young children. When caught, he was sent to the Provincial Asylum at Hildesheim for observation, and Dr Schmalfuss, who examined him there, considered him to be incurably feeble-minded and not responsible for his actions.

But Haarmaan showed some ingenuity when he

managed to escape from the asylum after six months, and made his way to Switzerland. There he lived by his wits – which meant in effect a life of daily petty crime.

After two years he returned to Hanover. There were violent rows between him and his father, which often ended in blows. The father became afraid of his son, although he did try to settle him down by buying him a fried fish shop. But Fritz soon made it bankrupt.

There was a period when Fritz was engaged to be married to a girl he had made pregnant, but she bore a stillborn child and he broke the engagement off. He enlisted in the 10th Jaeger battalion in Alsace, where he became an officer's batman. He was considered to be a very good soldier, full of *esprit de corps* and subservient in manner. But he was discharged after a few years, suffering from neurasthenia, and received a pension until his capture in 1924. Haarmaan later described his years in the army as 'the happiest time in my life'.

His return home meant more violent rows with his father, who tried to have his son certified. But Dr Andrae reported on 14 May 1903 that although Fritz was morally lacking, unintelligent and self-centred, these were not sufficient grounds to have him put in an asylum.

Haarmaan spent seven of the next twenty years in prison for burglary, fraud and indecency, and spent the entire period of the war behind bars. He was released in 1918 to find that the society which had condemned him was crumbling. Hanover was notorious for its homosexual community. In a city of some 450,000, there were five hundred male prostitutes known to the police, and the chief criminal inspector estimated the total number of homosexuals in Hanover at 40,000.

Haarmaan gravitated towards this group, hanging around the well-known homosexual taverns and dance-halls, where a gentleman could dance with a boy dressed as a girl all night long. He took lodgings at 27 Cellar-strasse, deep in the warren of narrow streets in the slum quarter. But what had attracted Haarmaan's immediate attention was the profusion of stalls outside Hanover railway station – a large Gothic building – all selling blackmarket goods and with no police interference.

He felt immediately at home in the vast square in front of the railway station, with its thousands of stalls selling everything from second-hand clothing, to cigarettes, chocolate, magazines and margarine, and meat of all description, from fish to fowl, beast to man. Most of the items on sale were stolen, and the stalls were operated by sharp and cunning rogues. But Haarmaan was an experienced criminal, an ex-convict who knew the scene. The whole world had turned criminal, and he was in his element.

He joined a meat-smuggling racket and soon lost his prison gauntness, putting on weight and, in his own words: 'I was like a stray cat adopted by a butcher.' Within six months he had his own business as a meat hawker, and had become a valued police informer, or *Spitzel*. He mixed freely at night with the transient population of runaways and crooks hiding out from the police. He always knew where anyone the police were interested in was to be found. He gave detailed reports on political meetings, and was never averse to turning in even his friends.

Not for cash – but for *immunity*. He could never have existed otherwise. As a result, the police turned a blind eye to his business transactions and his sexual preferences; and so deeply enmeshed with the police system did Haarmaan become that people began referring to him respectfully as 'Detective Haarmaan' – and they were not being sarcastic or ironic. They truly believed it. Every night – at midnight or later – he visited the railway waiting rooms, looking over the new crop of runaway boys and inspecting papers with an officious manner. He would listen to a boy's story of running away from a terrible home life, then offer him a meal and a bed in his own apartment. But only if he liked the look of the boy. There was a definite air of the official about him as he listened, head cocked to one side, to the stories of boys who were homeless and without any means of support. His expression was at once sympathetic and cynical – the look of policemen everywhere.

By day Haarmaan – who had been classified in his youth as being 'incurably feeble-minded' – flourished brilliantly. He always had meat when his competitors were out of supplies. People knew where to go for a good joint of meat. Nobody spotted the link between his night-time and day-time activities: the ready supply of meat, and the disappearance of young boys . . .

Haarmaan had committed his first murder. The victim was Friedel Rothe, born 1901, vanished 27 September 1918. How many followed is anyone's guess. When asked how many he had killed, Haarmaan himself was to say: '*Es können dreissig, es können vierzig sein; ich weiss das nicht* – thirty or forty, I can't remember.' He was to be formally convicted of twenty-four murders, those which the prosecution could *prove*.

The first victim, Rothe, was typical of all those who followed. His father was away at the front, a soldier defending the State. The boy hung around street corners, smoking and gambling, neglecting his schoolwork. One day he stole his father's civilian clothes and sold them to get money, then he ran away from home – to Hanover and the benevolent Detective Haarmaan. His mother received just one postcard from him, reading: *Dear Mother, It's more than two days since I ran away. But I will only come home if you promise to be nice to me. Affectionate greetings, your son Fritz.* Fritz met another Fritz who was really nice to him, but the young Fritz was never seen again.

When the father came home from the war, he and his wife began searching for their missing son, making inquiries of all his friends, and questioning the young male transvestites, who gave them information which led them to a young boy who had seen Fritz last. He said that Fritz had boasted of having made friends with a detective who gave him presents and took him for rides, then took him back to his rooms to smoke and chat. The boy knew the address: he had been there himself.

The clues led the parents to 27 Cellarstrasse, but they had to force the police to search the apartment of their valued informer. No clue to Friedel's whereabouts was found, but since the police caught Haarmaan in *flagrante delicito* with a young boy, they were forced to arrest their own spy, who was subsequently jailed for nine months for indecency. Four years later, when in custody, Haarmaan confessed that the head of the missing boy had been in his apartment at the time, wrapped in newspaper and hidden behind the stove.

Released in September 1919, Haarmaan moved to new quarters in Neustrasse. Soon afterwards he met another homosexual in the Café Kropcke, a haunt for sexual deviants. Hans Grans was twenty-four years younger than himself, but he was slim and coiled as a snake, and older in evil than Haarmaan. Grans was a pimp and petty thief, and as cunning and vicious as an alley rat. Together, Haarmaan and Grans made an unholy alliance.

The pattern was set; it was always the same. They enticed a homeless youth from the railway station to Haarmaan's apartment. The boy was sodomized and then killed – Haarmaan said by biting through his throat – and the body was then butchered and sold as meat at the local market stalls, and through other channels. The victims ranged from ten to twenty years of age, and some were killed simply because Grans wanted an item of their clothing.

Every evening boys left Haarmaan's apartment with carefully wrapped parcels of meat. No one thought anything of it. Haarmaan was, after all, a dealer in smuggled meat – a '*gehamstertes fleisch*'. Once he was seen coming from his apartment carrying a bucket covered with a cloth. When the cloth blew off to reveal that the bucket was full of blood, Haarmaan just whistled cheerfully and walked on. Again his trade allayed any suspicion.

Left: Gary Heidnik, the 'House of Horrors' killer, is escorted to court, April 4 1987. *(Popperfoto)*

Below: Police carry boxes containing human body parts out of Gary Heidnik's North Philadelphia home. They had earlier freed three women who had been imprisoned and shackled in the basement of the house by Heidnik. *(Popperfoto)*

Jeffrey Dahmer, charged with murdering and mutilating fifteen young men in Wisconsin, on his way to court, September 1992. *(Popperfoto)*

Above: Tracey Edwards – whose escape from Dahmer's apartment on July 22 1991, led to the latter's arrest – testifies about the night he went to Dahmer's home in Milwaukee. *(Popperfoto)*

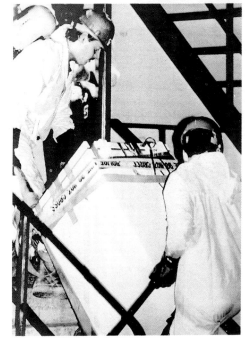

Right: Workers remove a refrigerator containing human heads from Dahmer's home, July 1991. Officials estimated that as many as eighteen victims were found in the apartment. *(Popperfoto)*

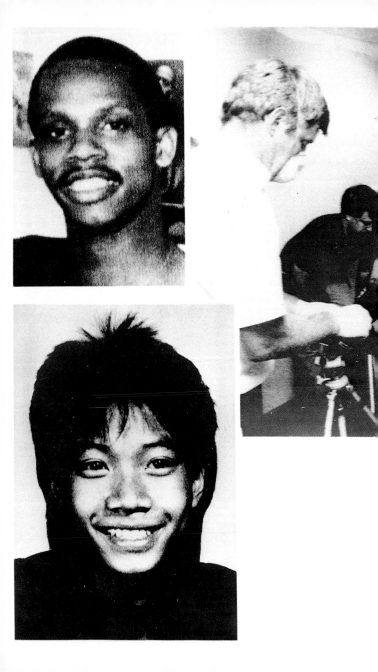

Above: Investigators search the den of Dahmer's boyhood home in Ohio. Police believed he committed his first murder there in 1978. *(Popperfoto)*

Top left and left: Two of Dahmer's victims: Oliver Lacy was found decapitated in Dahmer's kitchen, July 23 1991. Fourteen-year-old Konerak Sinthasomphone was last seen on May 27 1991, nude and bleeding outside Dahmer's apartment. *(Popperfoto)*

Right: Police identity portrait of Japanese student Issei Sagawa, charged with killing and dismembering Dutch student, Renee Hartwelt in 1981. Sagawa admitted eating some of her flesh. *(Popperfoto)*

Below: Sagawa leaving the Police Court, June 1981. *(Popperfoto)*

Left: Self-confessed serial killer Andrei Chikatilo stares through the bars of his courtroom cage during his trial for the murder of fifty-five people between 1979 and 1991. *(Popperfoto)*

Below: Chikatilo speaks in his own defence. In the outer courtroom, relatives of his victims bayed for his blood. *(Popperfoto)*

Chikatilo is led away by the local militia in Rostov, April 1992.
(Popperfoto)

One woman, who lived in the flat beneath Haarmaan, heard the noise of chopping one night and called out: 'Am I going to get a bit?' 'No, next time,' Haarmaan replied. Next day he brought her a sack of bones, but she said later: 'I made soup of them, but I thought the bones were too white, so I threw them away.'

Grans, the young lover of the ageing Haarmaan, was perhaps even worse than his master. He encouraged him, aided him, lived off the profits of his terrible trade. It was he who took the remains of the victims to the River Leine to dispose of them in the murky waters. Haarmaan was to complain that on at least two occasions Grans pushed him into abducting and murdering boys he didn't like the look of; he preferred to make his own selection, based on whether or not the victim was attractive to him.

From 1918 to 1923 there was no physical evidence of his murders – although there must have been many – but from February 1923 there were twenty-seven disappearances in which Haarmaan was definitely involved. The list is not comprehensive, but it is representative.

14 February 1923: Fritz Franke, 17. He had stolen from his parents' house in Berlin and run away. Some of his clothing was found in Haarmaan's possession. A curious feature of this case was that two women friends of Grans visited Haarmaan's apartment in his absence and found a large quantity of meat. They became suspicious and took a sample of it to the police. A police doctor reported that it was pork.

People were now beginning to suspect Haarmaan's cannibal activities, but his profession of police informer protected him to an incredible extent. When a police inspector set up in business as a private detective under the name of the Lasso Agency, he took Haarmaan in as a partner. Haarmaan now had credentials which certified him as a detective. Meanwhile, the list continued.

20 March 1923: Wilhelm Schulze, 17. His clothing was found in the possession of Haarmaan's landlady.

23 May 1923: Roland Huch, 15. His clothing was sold by Haarmaan.

May 1923: Hans Sennefeld, 20. His clothing was sold by Grans.

25 June 1923: Ernst Ehrenberg, 13. His canvas knapsack was found in the possession of Haarmaan.

24 August 1923: Heinrich Strus, 18. His possessions were found in Haarmaan's apartment.

24 September 1923: Paul Bronischewski, 17.

September 1923: Richard Graf, 17.

12 October 1923: Wilhelm Erdner, 16.

25 October 1923: Hermann Wolff. He used to loiter on the railway station, and boasted of having become friendly with a detective.

27 October 1923: Heinz Brinkmann, 13. His clothing was found in Haarmaan's possession.

23 November 1923: Adolf Hannappel, 17. Grans incited this murder for the boy's trousers.

6 December 1923: Adolf Hennies. His overcoat came into the possession of Haarmaan and Grans, and they had a quarrel over it which nearly brought their partnership to an end.

17 May 1923: Hans Keimes, 17. After he disappeared, his family received a visit from Haarmaan, who asked for a photograph of the youth, promising to find him 'within three days'. This was a curious incident. The boy was very handsome, and possibly Haarmaan coveted him as a lover. Shortly after the boy vanished, Haarmaan went to the police station to name Grans as his killer. Since Grans had been in custody when the boy disappeared, the matter was dropped, being dismissed as a homosexual lovers' quarrel. But the boy's body was found strangled and tied up in the canal – definitely not Haarmaan's style.

5 January 1924: Ernst Spiecker, 17. Grans was wearing the boy's shirt when arrested.

15 January 1924: Heinrich Koch. A young transvestite,

114

he spent a lot of time at the Bals Masques, dancing with gentlemen.

2 February 1924: Willi Senger, 20. His overcoat was found in Haarmaan's possession.

8 February 1924: Hermann Spiechert, 15.

6 April 1924: Alfred Hogrefe, 17.

April 1924: Hermann Bock, 23. A young thief who hung about the railway market, his murder was not typical of Haarmaan. The victim was older than the norm, and well able to take care of himself. Perhaps Haarmaan killed him as a rival in crime, and although he always denied this particular murder, Bock's clothing was traced to Haarmaan.

17 April 1924: Wilhelm Apel, 16.

26 April 1924: Robert Witzel, 18. His skull was found in the Leine. He liked to visit the Café Kropcke – without his parents' knowledge.

9 May 1924: Heinz Martin, 16. Haarmaan admitted this murder.

25 May 1924: Friedrich Abeling, 10. He was killed while playing truant.

26 May 1924: Fritz Wittig. Haarmaan said this murder was committed on the command of Grans.

5 June 1924: Friedrich Koch, 16. His possessions were found in Haarmaan's apartment.

14 June 1924: Erich de Vries, 17. He was lured to Haarmaan's apartment with the promise of free cigarettes.

And so the list goes on.

After his arrest Haarmaan said that he had never felt any fear, despite the fact that the paper-thin walls of his attic apartment were covered with layers of blood and despite his close shaves with the law. But he did claim to have felt remorse, telling of how he had once said to Grans: 'Hans, why am I different to other men? Perhaps I have two souls . . . ' But the remorse was not sufficient to prevent him from selling the clothing of his victims and disposing of their possessions as gifts to Grans, or at reduced prices to his landlady and her friends.

The discovery of his activities came about by accident. On 17 May 1924, small children playing on the banks of the Leine found a human skull. On the twenty-ninth another skull was found, and on 13 June two more skulls were seen in the mud. The police doctor had dismissed the skulls as being a practical joke by medical students. But when a sack full of human bones was found on 24 July, the police were forced to take the discoveries seriously.

Already there had been rumours of human flesh having been sold at the station market. Then there were all the boys who had disappeared, and now these new grisly finds . . . A wave of hysteria swept throughout Hanover – throughout Germany itself. As Bolitho noted: 'In Germany . . . socially the most advanced State in our civilization, the war series from band-music to man-eating was thus actually completed. In four years' action of the State . . . the days of werewolves and anthropophagi were brought back to Europe.'

The police decided to drag the Leine, and recovered some five hundred human bones. According to the police pathologist, these came from at least twenty-seven separate bodies, of children and young men.

Suspicion had already fallen on Haarmaan, but he was too friendly with the local detectives and knew them all by sight. Accordingly, the chief of police sent to Berlin for two experienced detectives to watch Haarmaan, and they kept him under observation at the railway station.

On the night of 22 June, Haarmaan was seen prowling among the sleeping men in the waiting rooms. A row suddenly broke out when he tried to arrest one man for travelling without a ticket. The man counter-charged Haarmaan with an act of indecency. The detectives took both men to the central police station.

With Haarmaan locked in a cell, the opportunity was taken to search his rooms, with the result that clothing and possessions belonging to many of the missing boys were found and identified. Haarmaan at first claimed that he came to have these items through his trade as a second-hand dealer; but after a period of brutal third-degree questioning, he confessed his crimes, naming Grans as his accomplice.

In his chilling confession he stated, in part:

I admit that I killed – possibly during the strange fits of madness that would overpower me at times – a number of youths whose names, with a few exceptions, escape me. I never really wanted to kill them. They were mostly poor boys, and I honestly took them home with the intention of sheltering and feeding them. But then we would get drunk and suddenly everything would go black. I would strangle them to death.

Haarmaan went on to say that he would then go to sleep, wake up later, brew some strong coffee and then dismember the bodies.

'I disposed of the useless parts of the corpses,' he added, 'and prepared the rest for sale.' The confessed murderer ended his statement with the fantastic admission: 'You see, gentlemen, I needed a million bodies.'

The trial of Haarmaan at Hanover Assizes on 4 December 1924 was a farce which lasted fourteen days, with one hundred and thirty witnesses being called. Haarmaan ruled the court; the judges pandered to his every whim, eager that he should 'behave' and confess everything, perhaps frightened that he might plead Not Guilty. When he complained of being bored and demanded to be allowed to smoke in the dock, they allowed him to light a cigar. When he complained that there were too many women in the court listening to such scandalous details, one of the judges apologized that he had no power to keep them out.

Haarmaan himself took over the questioning of some witnesses, urging them: 'Now come on. You must tell us all that you know. We are here to hear the truth.' The judges nodded their approval.

When Haarmaan denied a particular murder, his claim was immediately accepted without question and the jury instructed to find him not guilty of it. He denied having killed Hermann Wolff, for example, saying to the boy's parents: 'I have my tastes, after all. Such an ugly creature, according to his photograph, your son must have been, I would never have taken to. You say your boy had not even a shirt to his name. And his socks were tied on to his feet with string. *Pfui Deibel.* You ought to be ashamed to let him go about like that. Poor stuff like him there's plenty. Just think what you are saying. Such a youngster was much beneath my notice.'

Haarmaan was allowed remarkable latitude in the court, gabbling away gaily as he described biting through his victims' throats, laughing at odd moments. When Haarmaan rebuked a witness, the judges nodded assent. When he denied being mad or suffering from any nervous disorder, they nodded in agreement. They accepted everything he said unquestioningly, even to the extent of fawning on him, perhaps fearing that his links with the police would come out if he was opposed in any way.

There was no defence, no rebuttal of the evidence. Melodramatically and with a quiver in his voice, Haarmaan told the court: 'I want to be executed in the marketplace. On my tombstone must be put this inscription: "Here lies Mass-Murderer Haarmaan." On my birthday, Hans Grans must come and lay a wreath upon it.' He was listened to in silence, although his requests were not acceded to.

Finally Haarmaan was sentenced to be decapitated, while Grans was imprisoned for life. Haarmaan was aged fifty-four at the time of his execution, while his young lover-accomplice Hans Grans was twenty-four. (The sentence on Grans was later reduced to twelve years' imprisonment.) Haarmaan went to the guillotine in March 1925, but before his head was removed from his shoulders, he dictated a confession rivalling anything by De Sade. It was a full and descriptive account of every sexual perversion he had ever practised, along with an account of the pleasure he took from committing his murders.

Haarmaan was a frightening precursor of the Nazis.

7
KARL DENKE

Even as the trial of Haarmaan was progressing, there came news of the discovery of yet another cannibal-trader, this time from Munsterberg, in Silesia. 'Papa' Denke, as he was known locally, was a much respected citizen. He was the landlord of a large house in the town, and did some farming. He also played the organ in the local church every Sunday.

But post-war Germany was suffering from a famine, and hunger can turn scruples to ashes. Not that Denke *had* any scruples; what he did have was a keen commercial instinct for profit. Without any formal training in economics, he understood one of its basic laws: that of supply and demand. When a commodity is in short supply, its price rises. And he would not pay that higher price . . .

During the period 1921 to 1924, Denke was in the habit of killing vagrants and butchering their bodies into convenient-sized joints, which he kept pickled in brine.

His activities were brought to light when, on the evening of 21 December 1924, a coachman named Gabriel, who lived in the flat above Denke, heard loud cries for help. Fearing that his landlord was being robbed, he rushed downstairs to help, only to discover a young vagrant staggering about with blood pouring from a wound to his head. The man just had time to gasp that Denke had attacked him with an axe, before collapsing unconscious at the coachman's feet.

The coachman called the police, and Denke was

arrested. A search of his house revealed the identity papers of twelve vagrants, together with articles of their clothing in a sack. Two tubs of meat pickled in brine were found, as well as pots of fat and bones. Altogether police collected the remains of some thirty victims, both men and women.

A ledger was also found in which Denke, with Teutonic thoroughness, had written down the details of every carcass pickled, and the name, weight and date of death. It was another anticipation of Nazi bureaucratic methods.

Like Grossmann before him, Denke cheated justice. He committed suicide shortly after his arrest by hanging himself in his cell with his braces. Possibly his crimes were homosexual in origin, or motivated by hunger, but Denke was certainly a cannibal.

And what of the effects of such crimes on the general populace? We can only observe that during the mid-1920s schoolchildren in Germany told a joke which ran: 'Who is the world's worst murderer?' The correct answer was a pun: 'Haarmaan, *ich denke*' – which translates as: 'Haarmaan, I think.' Or 'Haarmaan, I, Denke.'

PART IV: CANNIBALISM FOR PLEASURE

1
ENTRÉE

Most crimes can be understood – if not forgiven – in terms of *motive*. In 1924 noted crime writer F. Tennyson Jesse gave us her six classic categories or motives for murder: gain, revenge, elimination, jealousy, lust and conviction. They remain pretty comprehensive, and valid for all time; and with a little mental effort we can enter the mind of the murderer, rapist, robber or dedicated assassin.

Even that most revolting of crimes, cannibalism, can be understood in terms of sheer necessity, or religious observance. Yet no amount of empathy can help one understand the eating of human flesh for sheer *pleasure*. The mere term itself is stomach-churning. The *pleasure* of cannibalism? There are some human activities which defy any rational explanation; the eating of human flesh for pleasure is one of them. Reading the case histories of such degenerates makes the mind reel with a kind of vertigo, as if peering down into a deep pit in which dark and slimy creatures slither just out of sight. It is a crime which negates every normal civilized impulse. But note that 'civilized' . . .

Fortunately, the true cannibal is rare, and people eating people is perhaps the most rare of all crimes. Necrophilia is far more common. However, as a human activity, cannibalism has a long pedigree – although it is still a current hobby with some people. One of the most recent people in England to come close to the definition of a cannibal was Denis Nilsen. Although he was never directly accused of eating any of his fifteen victims, he *did* mutilate and dismember their bodies, cooking them in his kitchen as an aid to disposal. Revealingly, perhaps, he wrote of his victims as 'the dirty platter after the feast', said that their flesh 'resembled meat in a butcher's shop', and described getting rid of the bodies as 'the washing-up'. All common references to the family dinner . . . The public anger and disgust over his handling of his victim's bodies genuinely puzzled Nilsen. He seemed unaware of any ethical code regarding corpses. For him they were not objects of veneration. This attitude could have been brought about by his training as a butcher and chef. A surprising number of killers have worked as butchers. The same sort of detachment from a corpse – viewing it as a piece of meat rather than a former person – can be seen in mortuary attendants, surgeons, pathologists, ambulancemen and hardened police officers.

And cannibalism continues. At the time of writing, a man in Japan is on trial for flesh-eating. The newspaper report appeared on 31 March 1990 and reads:

KIDNAP KILLER CONFESSES TO EATING CHILD VICTIM'S FLESH

A Japanese man charged with kidnapping and murdering four girls told a Tokyo court yesterday that he had eaten the flesh of one of his victims.

Tsutomu Miyazaki, 27, made the admission when he appeared before a judge for the first court proceedings since he was arrested in August last year.

Miyazaki admitted most of the charges put to him, but denied that the kidnap murders were premeditated. The ages of his victims ranged from four to seven.

'On the whole, my feelings [about the crimes] was that I did them in a dream,' he was quoted as saying.

Police said at the time of Miyazaki's arrest that his bedroom was filled with thousands of pornographic videotapes and comics.

The court heard that Miyazaki, who worked at his father's printing works, dismembered his victims' bodies and video-taped them.

The series of murders in and around Tokyo in 1988 and 1989 shook the whole nation.

Yesterday more than 1,500 people hoping to gain admittance queued outside the Tokyo district court building, but only 50 were allowed in.

The maximum penalty for murder in Japan is death. – Reuter.

Perhaps one of the first modern cannibals for pleasure was the infamous Jack the Ripper of 1888. He did, after all, send half a kidney he had removed from one of his victims to the chairman of the Whitechapel Vigilance Committee with a note declaring: 'T'other piece I fried and ate it was very nice.'

It is also from this same period, the nineteenth century, that we get the legend of Sweeney Todd. There are people who swear it is true, that they have seen the actual chair which used to swivel upside-down after the customer's throat had been cut, landing the body in the cellar, where it was butchered and made into pies. But it is all a myth.

It was actually a story published by Tom Prest under the title: *The String of Pearls: or The Sailor's Gift. A Romance of Peculiar Interest.* Later, when it became popular, it was known simply as *Sweeney Todd, the Demon Barber of Fleet Street.* In the story, the butchered corpses were handed over to Mrs Lovatt, who kept a cookshop next door much frequented by lawyers and their clerks. Mrs Lovatt's mutton pies were a favourite with them – until one day the awful truth came out when a customer found a finger in his pie . . .

More to the point is to ask: why *this* myth? Why did people so readily believe it to be a true tale? Was it a popular fear? Was it inspired by some real-life incident? Or is it the instinctive fear of us all: that we no longer know for certain what is in the pies we eat. We have to trust the makers . . .

But the history of this peculiar culinary taste goes back

much further than that. Perhaps the earliest recorded case is that of the Countess Elizabeth of Báthory, in 1611.

Born in Hungary in 1561, she was married at the age of fifteen to an aristocratic soldier, Count Ferencz Nadasy, and thus became mistress of the castle of Csejthe, in the Carpathians. Having been accustomed from birth to wealth and privilege, Elizabeth grew up to become a very bored and self-indulgent woman. She was in effect programmed to become a psychopath, with no feelings for others. She treated her servants appallingly badly, torturing them to get what she wanted: the immediate satisfaction of her own sensual needs. From her aunt she had learned of the sexual stimulus to be gained from whipping busty peasant girls.

Armed with a pair of special silver flesh-tearing pincers and a list of various tortures her husband had learned while fighting the Turks, she whiled away the lonely, idle hours. She was like a child tearing the wings off flies . . .

In 1604 her husband died, and she longed for a lover to replace him. But she was now forty-three, no longer a beauty, and men avoided her. Her longing for human blood came about by accident. One day she slapped the face of a servant girl so hard that she drew blood, a splash of which landed on her own face. When it was wiped off, the Countess was convinced that that part of her face was now much younger and fresher than the rest of her. She was convinced that she had discovered the elixir of youth.

For the next five years she dedicated herself to an orgy of blood, bathing every morning at four in virgin's blood, while her servants were out scouring the neighbourhood for more victims.

Later victims were killed by being shut in an iron maiden, a huge box moulded in the shape of a naked woman, hinged to open sideways and lined with sharp spikes. When the box was closed on the victim, the spikes pierced her body and the blood ran down into a special catchment area, to be gently warmed for the bath at daybreak. She also drank blood from the wounds of girls, and from the burn blisters of girls who were tortured and dying. According to the testimony of those girls who survived, 'some of their fellow victims were forced to eat their own flesh roasted on the fire. The flesh of other girls was chopped up fine like mushrooms, cooked and flavoured, and given to young lads who did not know what they were eating.'

The Countess had no difficulty in bullying the local Lutheran pastor to bury the mutilated and blood-drained bodies of her victims secretly in the village churchyard – sometimes as many as nine in one night. Other victims were merely thrown into local fields, the villagers believing they had been killed by some bloodsucking ghoul. But in time she exhausted the local supply of peasant blood, and became convinced that what she needed was aristocratic blood. Accordingly, in 1609 she advertised her willingness to take in twenty-five daughters of minor nobility for 'instruction in the social graces'.

Helped by her sinister peasant procuress Dorotta Szentes – known as 'Dorka' – she introduced the noble girls to the pleasures of torture. But she went too far. When four girls died under torture and their naked bodies were thrown over the castle walls, neighbouring peasants rescued the bodies before the wolves could take them, and identified them. The facts were reported to the authorities.

As an aristocrat, the Countess could not be arrested, so Parliament met and passed a new act just for her, and the militia raided the castle and arrested her.

A contemporary account of her arrest stated:

On 30 December 1610, the governor of the province, accompanied by soldiers, raided the castle and arrested everybody in it. They had interrupted an orgy of blood. In the main hall of the castle they found one girl drained of blood and dead, another living girl whose body had been pierced with holes, another who had just been tortured. In the dungeons and cellars they found and liberated a number of girls, some of whose bodies had already been pierced and 'milked', others intact, plump, well-fed, like well-fed cattle in their stalls. The dead bodies of some fifty more were subsequently exhumed.

The Countess had slaughtered, over the years, some six hundred young girls for her pleasure. The court records of her trial revealed the various methods she employed to harvest human blood. One was to 'put a terrified naked girl into a narrow iron cage furnished with pointed nails turned inwards, hang it from the ceiling and sit beneath it, enjoying the rain of blood which came down.'

She was tried at Bitce in 1611. The Lord Palatine of Hungary (her cousin) commuted the death penalty to one of life imprisonment, and ordered the Countess – 'this bloodthirsty and bloodsucking Godless women' – to be walled up in a small room in her castle, with only a tiny food-hatch linking her to the outside world. She took three-and-a-half years to die. Dorka, and others who had assisted the Countess in her wickedness, were burned alive after prolonged and public torture.

From the nineteenth century we have a couple of examples of this perverse desire to consume human bodies in one way or another. Antoine Langulet was brought up in the slums of Paris, and as a consequence of his back-street upbringing never developed a taste for normal food. He preferred his flesh to be rotten, even putrid – much as English gentlemen hang pheasants until they are 'gamy'.

Langulet developed into a nocturnal creature, sleeping by day in his attic, and emerging at night to pillage dustbins for anything edible they might contain. If he was lucky, he might find a dead cat in a gutter.

He progressed to a taste for human flesh and began robbing graves to satisfy his morbid hunger. Every time he watched a funeral, he must have thought it absurd to bury so much good food. His habit was to dig up the corpse and then cut open the stomach to reveal the intestines, which were his favourite delicacy. After feasting on these and filling his pockets with choice pieces of flesh, he would cover up the corpse for future use – as a kind of larder.

But like all criminals and fanatics, he went too far. He began taking the corpses home with him. And his depredations in the local cemeteries had not gone without notice.

Langulet found a newly buried young woman and dug her up, butchering her on the spot so that he could transport the meat more easily. He managed to carry the bulk of the corpse back to his room, but on his second trip with the remainder, he ran into a horrified gendarme and was arrested.

He was placed in the Bicetre Prison in Paris, where he confessed to his odd taste in food and seemed surprised that his activities had aroused any attention. What was all the fuss about? He did admit that his ideal meal, given a free choice, would be the tender flesh of a young child, but fear of the consequences had prevented him from ever committing murder.

'Congo' Pellé was a native of Haiti, and we owe our knowledge of the case to Her Britannic Majesty's consul-general there in the 1860s, who wrote an account of his experiences of the Vadoux – or voodoo – religion.

Sir Spenser St John was suspicious of most of the stories he heard, but he actually attended the trial of Pellé, who was well-versed in voodoo ceremony. Ambitious but with a dislike of hard work – it was said of Pellé: 'He was anxious to improve his position without any exertion on his own part' – he decided to make use of the voodoo powers of his sister, Jeanne. She declared that there would have to be a human sacrifice to achieve the desired results, and Pellé decided that his niece, Claircine, aged twelve, was the ideal choice.

Accordingly, during a magical ceremony on New Year's Eve, the girl was abducted and then strangled by a voodoo priest, Floréal, who afterwards decapitated her, allowing her blood to flow into a large earthenware pot.

Floréal then used a ritual knife to flay the girl's body, removing her skin entirely, before cutting the flesh from her bones to expose her skeleton. Her entrails were ceremoniously buried.

Then the worshippers proceeded in procession to Jeanne's house, singing a voodoo chant. Once at the house, the head and flesh were prepared for cooking, the head being steamed with yams to make one dish, the flesh steamed with congo beans to make another. Sir Spenser St John actually heard a witness, who had been spying on her neighbours through a crack in the wall, testify: 'I saw Jeanne cooking the flesh with congo beans, small and rather bitter, while Floréal put the head in a pot with yams to make some soup. While the others were engaged in the kitchen, one of the women present, Roséide Sumera, urged by the fearful appetite of a cannibal, cut from the child's palm a piece of flesh and ate it raw.' The night was then spent in an orgy of eating, drinking and sex, with the leftovers being cooked for breakfast.

The police came to learn of the affair from an informer, and fourteen people were arrested and strictly questioned, as a result of which eight of them were tried and found guilty of torture, sorcery and murder. Jeanne said that she had only been practising what had been taught her by her mother as the religion of her ancestors, and asked the judge: 'Why should I be put to death for observing our ancient customs?' They were all found guilty and sentenced to be executed by firing squad, and separated into pairs with five soldiers to shoot each pair. However, the soldiers were not very good shots, and they took thirty minutes to finish the prisoners off. But by the next morning, the graves of Jeanne and Floréal were already empty. Perhaps giving rise to the legend of the zombie, the walking dead . . .

2
FISH THE FREAK

The case of Albert Fish is a revolting one, and yet it is a valuable and instructive story. It illustrates the fact that such predatory psychopaths do lurk among us – like unseen sharks – and they generally look quite innocuous in appearance. But the great value of the Fish case is that it illustrates how a determined detective can get to the bottom of a mystery – even if it takes years and he has to devote his life to the case.

The lesson we can draw is that persistence in a detective is perhaps an even greater quality than the deductive ability of a Sherlock Holmes.

It began for Detective Will King as a routine missing person's report, but even then the background to the case was alarming enough.

On 28 May 1928, an old man knocked at the door of a basement apartment at 406 West 15th Street in the seedy Chelsea district of Manhattan.

The caller said he was looking for the man who had advertised for a job in the *New York World Telegram*. Giving his name as Frank Howard, the old man explained that he owned a farm at Farmingdale, Long Island, and would be willing to pay fifteen dollars a week for a good worker.

The man who had advertised for work was Edward Budd, the eighteen-year-old son of Albert Budd, who was finding it hard to support his wife and four children on a doorman's wage. The family were delighted with the job offer, but the mild-looking old man said he would return a week later for a firm decision. He failed to keep the appointment, but sent a telegram apologising for having been unavoidably delayed.

In fact he arrived the next day, Sunday, 3 June 1928, bearing a gift for Mrs Budd: a pail of pot cheese. He was expensively dressed, and flashed a wallet stuffed with dollar bills. This in itself was rare in the poverty-stricken late twenties in New York.

The old man had dinner with the family, then gave the eldest children money to go to the cinema. After talking expansively for a while, the old man kindly offered to take the ten-year-old daughter, Grace, to a birthday party at the house of his married sister at 137th Street off Columbus Avenue.

The parents gave their permission without hesitation, and Grace went off, trustingly holding the old man's hand, dressed in her white communion dress. She was never seen alive again.

When she failed to return home by next morning, the parents went to the police, who were able to tell them that there was no such address as that given by the old man: Columbus Avenue only went as far as 109th Street. Further checking revealed that there was no 'Frank Howard' who owned a farm in Long Island, and neither was there any clue to his identity, since he had taken back the telegram he had sent to the Budd family.

Detective Will King of the Missing Persons Bureau took on the case as a personal challenge, and the first thing he did was to trace the original telegram form which 'Howard' must have filled in by hand at the post office. It took two clerks thirteen hours to find it among thousands of forms. It had been sent from the East Harlem branch of Western Union, but since it would have been impossible to search every house in that district for the missing child, King set out instead to trace where the pail of pot cheese had been sold. Every store in Harlem was traced and eliminated before King found the street hawker who had sold it. He gave an accurate description of the old man, but that was of little help.

There was intense newspaper and radio publicity about the abducted child, which resulted in hundreds of crank letters but no real clues. After a few months the police were forced to abandon the search as hopeless. The trail had gone cold. But Detective King refused to give up and devoted his career to finding the child or her killer.

The years went by. Then, on 11 November 1934, Grace Budd's mother received a macabre letter. Naturally, it was anonymous. The writer said that a friend of his, a Captain Davis, had acquired a taste for human flesh while in China, where children were being eaten during a famine. On returning to New York, Davis had kidnapped two small boys and beaten them 'to make the flesh good and tender', then killed and eaten them.

The writer went on to say that he had decided to try it for himself, and so had abducted Grace, taking her to a house in Westchester.

He described stripping himself naked, then strangling the child, before cutting her into pieces and taking her home to cook and eat her.

It might have been a letter from De Sade himself, and the effect on the mother can only be imagined.

The father took the letter to the police. Detective Will King was still on the case; he had declined to retire two years earlier, still determined to track down the killer of Grace Budd. Now he had his second clue. The first had been the telegram form signed *Howard*. A comparison of the handwriting on the two items showed them to have been written by the same man.

The flap of the envelope which had contained the letter carried a design which had been partially blacked-out with ink. Under the spectroscope it proved to be the letters NYPCBA. King deduced that the letters stood for New York Private Chauffeurs Benevolent Association, which had its headquarters at 627 Lexington Avenue.

King spent several hours at the association's office,

comparing the handwriting of every employee with that on the letter, but found that none of the four hundred-odd samples matched. King then addressed the assembled employees. Had any of them taken the Association's stationery for personal use?

One man, a chauffeur called Lee Siscoski, admitted that he had, saying he had left some envelopes in his room at 622 Lexington. King hurried to that address, but found no envelopes there. Then Siscoski recalled that he had previously rented a rom at 200 West 52nd Street. He might have left them there . . .

This was a boarding house, and when Detective King described 'Howard' to the landlady, she nodded in recognition. 'That sounds like the man in number seven – Albert Fish,' she said.

The signature of Albert Fish in the register matched the handwriting of the man who had written both the telegram and the letter. Naturally, Detective King was anxious to talk to the man. The landlady said that Fish had moved, but he would be back sometime to collect the monthly cheque sent to him by one of his sons. Another officer might have asked the landlady to telephone the police the next time Fish showed up, but Detective King rented a room in the boarding house and sat down to wait.

It was three weeks before Albert Fish arrived on the scene. King arrested him without any fuss, but on the way to the police station the old man turned nasty, lungeing at King with an open razor in each hand. King grabbed him by his wrists, banging them against a wall to make him drop the razors, and then handcuffed him. When he searched his prisoner, he found his pockets to be full of knives and razors.

Fish confessed to the murder of Grace Budd immediately, and described it in detail. Police took Fish back to his house, Wisteria Cottage, in Worthington Woods, and found the bones of Grace Budd. Also in Fish's house police made another interesting discovery: he had a large collection of newspaper cuttings about the exploits of a certain Fritz Haarmaan in Germany . . .

Back at police headquarters, Fish at first denied having committed any other murders, but finally told his story of four hundred child murders committed between 1910, when he was forty, and 1934. This figure was never verified, but it is certain that Fish killed dozens of children over a twenty-four-year period.

Fish had left school at fifteen to work in a grocery store, but soon left to become an apprentice painter and decorator. This was a trade which allowed him to travel across the country, and of necessity brought him knowledge of empty buildings and cellars. It was an ideal background for a sex-pervert.

Fish told detectives that when he was on a painting job he was always nude beneath his overalls, and when he came into contact with a young boy he would expose himself.

Many of his victims were poor children from the urban ghettos. Sometimes Fish would pay boys to procure him other children, and his sexual activities had taken place in twenty-three separate states of the Union.

There had been some near escapes. He had nearly been captured in St Louis with a small boy he had been torturing for days. There was a narrow squeak in Virginia, another in Delaware, and several in New York. He was questioned several times when children disappeared, but the small old man was never a serious suspect.

Fish got married at the age of twenty-eight to a nineteen-year-old girl and they had six children, but after twenty years she ran away with the lodger. Fish raised the children on his own, despite the fact that his errant wife had sold all the furniture in their apartment to finance her departure.

His sexual proclivities were weird in the extreme, although his children became used to them. He enjoyed sticking needles into his scrotum, or spanking himself with a nail-studded wooden paddle. Sometimes he got

138

children to flay him until he bled. His own children had seen him beating himself, but they assumed he was merely eccentric.

Why did Fish like children as victims? Because of their innocence, and because – as he smirked to detectives – 'they don't talk'. It was certain that the children he had murdered over all those years never told.

It was almost seven years after Grace Budd's murder that Fish stood trial in Westchester County, New York State. The court was packed with over twenty reporters. The district attorney rose to his feet to make his opening address.

'May it please the court, Mr Foreman and gentlemen of the jury. The defendant, Albert Howard Fish, is charged with murder in the first degree, in that he choked to death one Grace Budd, in the town of Greenburgh, in this county.'

The spectators gazed at the sixty-five-year-old man sitting in the dock, looking so meek and innocent. Could he really have been such a sexual pervert, cannibal and monster of the worst degree?

The district attorney continued: 'The people will prove that the defendant, on his own admission, appeared at the apartment of Albert Budd, the victim's father, on the afternoon of June third 1928, and took his daughter Grace, then a child not eleven years old, away with him to Greenburgh, to an unoccupied house known as Wisteria Cottage, where he choked the life from her.

'Nothing has been seen of Grace Budd from that day to this. When the defendant took her away that afternoon, ostensibly to a party at his sister's, her fate was sealed. Despite urgent police enquiries, no trace of her could be found for over six years until a letter arrived at the Budds' home on 11 November 1934, addressed to Mrs Budd.'

The district attorney took an envelope from his brief-case. 'With the court's permission, I will read this letter to the jury. It is, gentlemen, unsigned, but you will hear evidence that it, and the envelope it came in, has been traced to the defendant.'

He read an expurgated version of the letter.

Slamming the letter down with obvious disgust, the district attorney called his first witness. Detective Will King took the stand. 'You are a detective attached to the New York City police force?'

'Yes, sir.'

'Then tell us of the events of December thirteenth last, and what led up to them.'

Speaking in a firm voice, Detective Will King said: 'When Mrs Budd received the letter she contacted me at once. I had been originally assigned to the case, and the file remained open. From an imperfectly erased address on the back of the envelope, I managed to trace the defendant to an apartment on 52nd Street. I arrested him and took him down to headquarters, where he voluntarily made a statement.'

'What was in the statement?'

'Well, sir, he said he had left a bundle containing a butcher's knife, a cleaver and a saw by the newsstand on the corner of the Budds' apartment block. After he had taken the Budd child away he travelled with her on the E1, and then on the New York Central to Greenburgh. They left the train together and went to a house there known as Wisteria Cottage. He said that he took her into a room there, and that he choked her to death. The choking took about five minutes.

'Then, sir, he took off her clothes and cut her head off with the cleaver. Then he sawed her in two across the body above the navel and left the lower part of the body behind the door in the room. The head he wrapped in paper and hid behind the cistern in the outside lavatory.

'Three or four days later, he cannot remember which, he returned to the house and threw all three sections of the body over the stone wall that runs behind it. After making the statement he was taken to the spot where he

140

said the body lay, and we found the bones of a young female, aged about ten, cut off just as he had described.'

The district attorney held out a cardboard box which had been entered as an exhibit. Taking off the lid, he said: 'Would these be the bones, officer?'

'Yes, sir. I recognise the official label.'

The district attorney put the box down, then asked: 'Did the defendant afterwards add anything to the statement?'

'Yes, sir,' the detective replied. 'In all he made six formal confessions to the murder while in our custody, adding details as the confessions went along. He also said that he was sorry he had killed her, and that he would have done anything to bring her back to life.'

Against all that weight of evidence, there was only one plea which counsel for Fish could enter: insanity.

Dr Wertham, one of America's top psychiatrists, had been asked to examine Fish in jail, and Fish came to like and trust him. Later, Dr Wertham was to devote a chapter in his book *The Show of Violence* to Albert Fish. He wrote that although Fish looked meek and inoffensive, he was 'the most complex example of the polymorphous pervert I have ever encountered'. Fish practised every known form of sexual deviation from sodomy to sadism to eating human excrement. Under X-ray, several needles years old were discovered in his body. Fish even enjoyed inserting cotton wool soaked in alcohol into his anus and setting it alight. Wertham was convinced that Fish was insane.

Fish suffered from 'religious insanity', defending the castration of boys as symbolic of Abraham's biblical sacrifice of Isaac. He had visions of Christ and His Angels, as well as hell, and believed himself to be a particularly holy man – even God. He felt driven to torture and kill children . . . He felt that he was commanded by God to castrate little boys, so wrote Wertham. Fish himself declared: 'I had to offer a child for sacrifice, to purge myself of iniquities.'

Raised in an orphanage where he was badly treated, Fish once wrote: 'Misery leads to crime. I saw so many boys whipped that it ruined my mind.' He actually viewed his killing of chidren as an act of mercy to save his victims from the horror of life.

On the witness stand Dr Wertham said that initially he had seen Fish as a meek and innocuous little old man. But during many interviews he had come to the conclusion that he was dealing with the most prolific child-killer in American history.

'He has told me that he feels driven to torment and kill children. Sometimes he would gag them, tie them up and beat them, though he preferred not to gag them as he liked to hear their cries. In this case his original intention was to take Grace's brother and castrate him – he claims he is ordered by God to castrate small boys – but Edward Budd was too large.

'Instead he took Grace. He explained that he had to sacrifice her to prevent her from future outrage in the adult world. He felt that this was the only way in which she could be saved. That is why he killed her.

'On the day of the murder when they arrived at the house, he took his implements outside and stripped. The child was out in the sunshine picking flowers. He went to the window and called out to her; when she came in and saw him naked she screamed that she would tell her mother. He grabbed her by the throat, threw her to the floor, and strangled her. It was, he says, "to put her out of her misery".

'He took parts of the body home with him and cooked them in various ways. Then, over a period of nine days, he ate the flesh by day and thought about it by night, during all which time he was in a state of intense sexual excitement.'

The effects of this testimony on the jury was evident: they shuddered. In those far-off days of the 1930s, crime was a relatively innocent thing. The doings of Fish were like something out of a nightmare.

Dr Wertham went on to relate the many crimes which Fish had confessed to him – at least one hundred forced seductions of young boys with whose bodies he had enjoyed repugnant and perverted sexual acts. He concluded with his opinion that Fish was insane.

However, the prosecution had four psychiatrists willing to state that Fish was completely sane; the perversions he practised were common in the community. 'A quarter of the people walking the streets are psychopaths,' one expert declared.

Dr Wertham was cross-examined remorselessly. 'Tell me, doctor, insanity is a disease of the mind, is it not? If the defendant knows the difference between right and wrong he is not insane?'

In vain did Dr Wertham protest that knowing the difference between right and wrong was far too simplistic. The McNaughten Rules were out of date . . . It was the old controversy between the legal and medical professions. The law demanded a simple test: the ability to know right from wrong. Dr Wertham argued that a man might know that, yet still be insane, unable to control his terrible urges.

The prosecution conceded all the points raised by Dr Wertham. Fish *was* a pervert. He *did* eat human excrement – but so did many people prominent in public life. He had eaten Grace Budd's flesh and derived sexual satisfaction from the act of cannibalism. He did like to bind and castrate small boys. *Nevertheless, he was still sane*.

In his closing speech the prosecutor poured scorn on the idea that Fish might be insane; as far as he was concerned Fish was just another common criminal, a brutal killer who deserved the chair. But he had carefully neglected to call the psychiatrist who had been in charge of Fish during his many stays at New York's psychiatric hospitals: the one expert who could have testified to Fish's gross abnormality.

The jury were unimpressed with the psychiatric

evidence anyway; they had witnessed a monster who deserved to be put to death, a human freak. They found Fish guilty of murder in the first degree. Fish smiled as the judge passed the death sentence upon him.

Fish was on Sing Sing's death row when his appeal was heard. Dr Wertham repeated his original evidence. The chief judge admitted that 'there is no doubt that this man is insane', but went on to say: 'But the question which has to be answered is this: does he come within the legal definitions of insanity?' The Court of Appeals found that he did not, and confirmed the death penalty on Fish.

A direct appeal was made to the state governor. The district attorney said bluntly: 'I cannot see one single fact that deserves leniency on your part.'

Dr Wertham, eloquent in his defence of Fish, said: 'This man is not only incurable and unreformable, but *unpunishable*. In his own distorted mind he is looking forward to the electric chair as the final experience of supreme pain.'

The legal adviser sitting with the Governor nodded assent. 'To execute a sick man is like burning witches,' he commented. The Governor did not appear to be impressed with this line of argument.

Dr Wertham said passionately: 'I am not appealing to you as a politician, a lawyer, or anything else – I am appealing to you as a man.' The Governor and his staff left the room to reflect, then came back with a denial of clemency. Fish must die . . .

In his death cell, Fish appeared oblivious to all this. He was showing signs of increasing excitement. The 'Moon Maniac', as the newspapers had dubbed him – since most of his killings took place at or around full moon – told reporters that he welcomed going to the electric chair as 'the supreme thrill. The only one I haven't tried'.

The warden of Sing Sing, Lawes, waited all day in his office on the final day, hoping for a call from the

144

governor's mansion in Albany granting a reprieve. It never came.

As Fish was led into the execution chamber he smiled in confusion and told reporters: 'I don't know what I'm doing here.' They reported that he looked 'positively joyful'. Once in the chair, Fish helped adjust the electrodes as he was being strapped in. All those needles in his body caused trouble when the current blasted through him. They short-circuited. The first jolt of electricity failed to kill him, and he had to be given a second jolt. Witnesses reported seeing a puff of blue smoke above his head before the second charge extinguished him.

The story of the needles causing a short-circuit and thus making a second jolt may be apocryphal – it is normal practice to give the condemned two jolts – but what is certain is that Fish himself denied being insane. He told reporters: 'I am not insane. I am just queer. I don't understand myself.'

It was on 16 January 1936 that Fish went to his death. Fish, the cannibal of New York, had been roasted by official decree.

It is typical that Fish should be remembered so long after his terrible deeds, while the name of the detective whose patience and determination brought him to justice is forgotten. Detective Will King deserves better than oblivion.

3

GEIN THE GARGOYLE

It was the custom in medieval times to carve devils and imps along church façades, either to remind the congregation of the perils of hell, or to ward off evil spirits. Edward Howard Gein was a human gargoyle, sent to frighten us all. And like a gargoyle carved from stone, he was cold, remote, unfeeling. He was also the real-life killer on whom author Robert Bloch based the character Norman Bates in his classic novel: *Psycho*.

Plainfield is a small town in the middle of the huge flat plains of central Wisconsin, in the American Midwest. In the 1950s the town's only recreation was hunting. It boasted a cinema, of course, and a hamburger joint, but most men tended to hang around Hogan's Tavern. The bar was owned and operated by Mary Hogan, a large busty woman with a shady reputation. She was a mysterious character. All that was known about her was that she had been married twice and wouldn't take crap from any man. She was a hard-bitten, dominant woman of the world.

Some said she had connections with the Mob, others that she had formerly run a brothel in Chicago and had retired, buying the tavern with her profits. Whatever else she was, she was certainly a talking-point in the deeply conservative and God-fearing community. Men tended to be drawn to her by the hint of something illicit; women disapproved of her.

On 8 December 1954 she vanished. A farmer came into the tavern for a drink to take the chill of a freezing

146

winter's day. He found the door open but the bar deserted. He called out loudly for service but got no reply. Then he noticed a large patch of blood behind the counter, in the passage leading to the back room. He called the police immediately.

Sheriff Harold S. Thompson was quickly on the scene, along with his deputies. An examination of the bar revealed that something – or someone – had been dragged through that patch of blood towards the front door. There was a spent cartridge from a .32 calibre rifle. Mary Hogan had vanished but her car was still parked in its usual place. Outside the tavern, the sheriff spotted fresh tyre-marks in the snow, obviously made by a pick-up truck of some kind. It appeared that Mary Hogan had been shot dead, and her body taken away.

But why? There was no evidence of either a struggle or a motive. The cash register had not been touched. Had something from her past caught up with her? Had she been killed by a Mob hit-man? Despite a large-scale search of the area nothing was found and the case remained unsolved.

But local people were already talking about other unexplained disappearances. In May 1947 an eight-year-old girl, Georgia Weckler, had vanished after coming home from school. In November 1952 two farmers, Victor Travis and Ray Burgess, set out on a hunting trip. They never returned. They too had vanished and their bodies were never found. In 1953 fifteen-year-old Evelyn Hartley vanished while baby-sitting for a neighbour. Although her bloodstained clothing was found near the highway, her body was never recovered. What had happened to all these people?

Gradually the fear which had gripped the town died down with the passing of time. People still talked about it casually, but it was something from the past: safely remote.

Living alone on a farm six miles west of Plainfield was a reclusive man in his fifties, called Ed Gein. He had lived there since childhood, and following the death of his mother in 1947, continued to scrape an existence by hiring himself out as the local handyman. He grew nothing on his farm, which he had inherited as a two hundred and seventy-five acre property from his father in 1940, and which had lain fallow ever since. He had gradually sold off parcels of land until 1957 when only one hundred and sixty acres remained, and he was negotiating to sell more of his land to a neighbouring farmer. His needs were simple, but he needed cash for the beer he drank and for the pulp magazines he read avidly.

Although hard-working, the balding man with the pale blue eyes was regarded as something of an eccentric in the community. He did not join in casual conversation or engage in gossip. He was a quiet and reserved man. One neighbour happened to mention to him that Mary Hogan was still missing. Gein made an enigmatic reply which was typical of him. 'She ain't missing,' he mumbled. 'She's up at the farm right now.' The neighbour took it to be a macabre attempt at humour.

Gein was known to have at least three shrunken heads in his house, which he had shown to a cousin, claiming that they had been given to him by a man who had fought in the Philippines during World War II and brought them back as a souvenir.

At the start of the 1957 hunting season in Plainfield, an announcement was made that a cash prize would be awarded to the man bringing back the biggest buck with a set of antlers. The judge was to be Bernard Muschinski, who kept a garage in the town, which had a large weighing machine. On the night of Friday, 15 November 1957, he noticed Ed Gein drive by in his pick-up truck. Gein even waved to him.

Gein parked his truck in front of the general store, which Bernice Worden had run since the death of her husband in 1931, with the help of her son, Frank, a deputy sheriff. She sold everything from farm implements to rifle ammunition. Gein bought some ice-cream, then ordered some anti-freeze, saying he would be by to pick it up the following day. He asked Frank if he would be at the store, but Frank replied that he would be out hunting, competing for that prize money.

Saturday, 16 November dawned, and most of the town was deserted, with the men out hunting. Bernice Worden was alone in her store, not expecting much custom. At 8.30 a.m. Ed Gein appeared in the doorway, carrying a glass jar. Mrs Worden filled it with anti-freeze and wrote out a sales slip. Gein then took down a hunting rifle from the rack on the wall, explaining that his old weapon was not much good. He fiddled about with it, and when Mrs Worden wasn't looking, he slipped a cartridge into the breech and shot her in the head at point-blank range.

What happened next can only be pieced together from eyewitnesses. Between 8.45 and 9.30 a.m., Bernard Muschinski noticed Mrs Worden's delivery van pull out from behind her shop and head out of town. Gein was next seen by Elmo Ueeck, who had just shot a deer on Gein's land and was expecting Gein to get angry about it. But Gein just drove by fast in his Ford car, giving a friendly wave.

Around noon Ueeck called at the farm to apologize to Gein, but Gein was busy changing the tyres on his car and told Ueeck not to worry. He would settle for some of the venison.

In the afternoon two young neighbours asked Gein if he would drive them into town to buy a new battery; their car had broken down. Gein stepped out of his house, his hands dripping with blood. He explained that he was dressing a deer. The couple – teenager Bob Hill and his sister Darlene – were puzzled. Gein had always expressed an aversion to butchery. But Gein drove them to town, where Hill's mother, who ran a grocery store, invited him to stay for supper. Gein accepted the invitation eagerly.

While Gein was still in the Hills' house eating supper, Bernice Worden's son arrived back at the family store to find the place closed up and locked. He was puzzled when Muschinski told him about having seen his mother's delivery van on the road that morning. She had no deliveries to make that he knew of . . .

He opened the door to the shop and immediately noted that the cash register was missing, wrenched from its place on the counter. At the back of the shop he found a large pool of blood. He immediately telephoned County Sheriff Art Schley at Wautoma, some fifteen miles away. Art Schley was thirty-two years of age and had been made sheriff just that year. This was to be his first murder case.

Sheriff Schley arrived at the store, with a deputy, twenty minutes later. In the meantime, Frank had been searching the shop and had found the sales slip made out to Ed Gein. When the sheriff arrived Frank told him: 'My mother had only one customer today – Ed Gein.' The Sheriff agreed that they should go out and have a word with Gein, but first he wanted to take a look around the store. He noticed that in the gun rack, which held several weapons of different calibres, one rifle had been taken out and replaced back to front. He took it down and sniffed the barrel. It had been fired recently. It was bagged for evidence.

Two police officers, Dan Chase and Deputy Spees, had been alerted to keep an eye out for Gein, and arrested him at the Hills' home, where he was enjoying his supper. Meanwhile, Sheriff Schley drove with Frank to Gein's farm, only to find it dark and unoccupied. The Sheriff decided to take a look around, and both men entered the kitchen-extension at the rear of the house – more properly a wood out-building – flashing their torches.

They found an abattoir, but all the carcasses hanging up were human. A woman's headless body greeted them, with a huge hole in the stomach where all the internal organs had been removed. It was hanging upside down from a branch which had been driven through the tendons of both ankles. Although the body was naked and headless, Frank recognized it as being his mother, from a large mole on her left forearm. He ran outside, retching.

Sheriff Schley probed further and found Mrs Worden's head sitting on a shelf, wrapped in plastic, staring at him. The face wore a particularly peaceful expression. He went outside in the fresh air, where Frank grabbed him by the arm and said: 'I'm going home for my shotgun and then I'm going to find Ed. Then you can arrest me for murder too!'

Schley shook Frank, convincing him that the best way of dealing with the situation was to bring Gein to justice and let the electric chair take care of him. He drove the sobbing Frank back to town in his patrol car.

He discovered that Gein had been arrested. He also learned that Gein had made a significant remark at the time of arrest. When asked to account for his movements that day, he had said: 'Somebody framed me.'

'Framed you for what?' He was asked.

'Well, about Mrs Worden.'

'What about Mrs Worden?'

'Well, she's dead, ain't she?'

Early on the Sunday morning Gein's farmhouse – which was a pigsty of a place, with rotting garbage and filth everywhere, and dirty unwashed plates and rusty cans in every room as though an animal lived there – was searched by technicians from a mobile crime laboratory based in Madison, the state capital.

A generator was brought in to power arc-lights to illuminate the chamber of horrors they found inside the out-house. Parts of at least twelve human female bodies were found, together with human skulls on a shelf. A cardboard box held human noses, and on the stove was a pan of water containing a human heart, ready for cooking. Mrs Worden's heart . . .

Some skulls had been sawn in half to be used as drinking vessels. And human remains had been used as furniture. A chair seat had been covered in strips of human skin; also made from human skin were a lampshade,

151

waste-paper basket, drum, bracelet, and the sheath of a hunting knife.

Skin had been used to make 'leggings', and Gein had found a way to make genuine shrunken heads by peeling off the face and scalp of his victims and stuffing them with newspaper. He had nine of them, all with their hair intact. Some had been treated with oil to keep them supple, others showed traces of lipstick. And one of those shrunken heads was recognized as being that of Mary Hogan, the woman who had vanished three years before.

The police officers and forensic technicians were sick with horror. Nothing in their experience had prepared them for what they saw now. The entrails of Bernice Worden were found wrapped in an old suit. Her head had had two hooks thrust through its ears by which to hang it up on the wall – the ultimate trophy in a hunting state.

The house was a virtual mausoleum. Nothing had been changed since the death of Gein's mother twelve years previously. Old newspapers, half-eaten meals – everything remained as she had left it. Almost as if he expected her to return . . .

The corpse of Bernice Worden and the other human remains were taken away to the police morgue for autopsy and examination.

Perhaps the most significant find was a pile of newspaper clippings inside the covers of a book, detailing the case of a GI who had had a sex-change operation. There were also stacks of pulp magazines everywhere, detective mysteries and pornographic books and magazines. There were 'true life' detective magazines with explicit photographs of bodies, and horror comics with titles like *Tales From the Crypts* – the equivalent of today's video nasties. On bookshelves were many volumes dealing with Nazi atrocities and the exploits of cannibals. All this material had served to fuel Gein's sick fantasies, and was ammunition for those claiming that pornography could influence people to kill.

While the grim discoveries at his farmhouse were being examined, Ed Gein sat in the Wautoma county jail. He was questioned for twelve hours non-stop without an attorney present, but refused to answer any questions. The autopsy on Bernice Worden revealed that she had died from a .32 bullet to the head.

On Monday, 18 November, Gein broke down. He made a full confession, detailing how he had shot Mrs Worden, bundled her body into the back of her delivery van and driven it out of town to a pine forest where his own car waited. He had then transferred the corpse to his car, driving the body back to his house to truss it up and butcher it. District Attorney Earl Kileen issued a press statement including the details from Gein's confession.

The questioning of Gein continued. He could not clearly remember killing Mrs Worden, since he had been 'in a daze'. Asked why he had taken the cash register, he explained it was so that he could strip it down and see how it worked – just as he had with the bodies.

Gein said he used to dress the bodies as hunters dress deer, by hanging them up by the feet and slitting open the stomach to remove the entrails. He also removed the brains from the skulls. Pressed to explain where the other human remains had come from and how many women he had killed, Gein insisted that he had only killed once – Mrs Worden – and that had been an accident. All the other bodies found at his farm he had stolen from graves. He even gave names from tombstones.

He told of how over the past few years a compulsion to rob graves had seized him, particularly if he had known the deceased in life. (Among the books on his shelves was one about Burke and Hare, the Edinburgh body-snatchers.)

He explained that following a funeral in the town, he would drive to the cemetery that night and retrieve the freshly buried body, leaving the grave in 'apple-pie order'.

On the Monday Gein was given a polygraph test and

questioned about other murders. The results were inconclusive; but he had certainly murdered more than once – the head of Mary Hogan found at his farm was proof of that.

When wired up to the polygraph in the State Central Crime Laboratory at Madison, Gein was subjected to nine hours of questioning, during which he confessed that he had often dressed in the skins of his victims, and 'might' have murdered Mary Hogan – he said he was very hazy about the details. The killing of Bernice Worden, which he admitted, had been an accident, he claimed.

Giving details of his grave-robbing expeditions, Gein said that if the soil was loose enough, he removed it by hand and then opened the coffin lid with a crowbar to get at the corpse. He might take just the head, sawing it off across the neck. On other occasions he removed internal organs. Sometimes he took the entire body. But all the bodies were female, and he always replaced the coffin lid and refilled the grave neatly.

He said: 'I'd read the obituary notices in the papers, then I'd go to the cemetery in the middle of the night and dig up the body. No one saw me go, or come back. I had a compulsion to do it. It all started after my mother died in 1945. I felt I wanted to change my sex and become a woman. I used to skin the bodies and wear the skin. I'd make a mask from the face. Then I felt I was really like the woman I wanted to be. I liked to wear women's hair, too – I'd wear a scalp like a wig. I enjoyed cutting up bodies and sorting out the inside parts too. Once I made a vest out of a woman's skin. I'd oil the skins and faces to prevent them from drying out. I'd wear them around the house . . . '

On Thursday, 21 November, Gein was formally charged with the murders of Bernice Worden and Mary Hogan. When he appeared in court the following day for a preliminary examination, his lawyer pleaded insanity on his behalf, and the judge committed Gein to the

Central State Hospital for the Criminally Insane for examination.

Meanwhile, the police concentrated on Gein's grave-robbing expeditions. The results of the polygraph test indicated that he had been telling the truth about this, and when the graves he had specifically mentioned were opened, the coffins were found to be empty. In one coffin police found a steel crowbar. No one knew how many other graves in Plainfield Town Cemetery had been similarly violated, and the decision was taken not to examine any more to spare the feelings of relatives.

The psychiatric report on Gein concluded that he was schizophrenic, his early history indicating that his condition had begun in childhood.

Gein was born on 27 August 1906 to Augusta Gein, a stern, religious woman who hated her husband, the drunken George Gein. She often wished he were dead, and said so in the presence of her son. She frequently got down on her knees to pray for her husband to die.

The mother brought up Gein to do without friends. All outside influences were viewed as a threat to his moral purity, and she was constantly preaching the scriptures at him, reminding him that all men were sinners. In fact, the mother had developed a loathing of men.

Gein's father died in 1940. His mother suffered a stroke in 1944, and Gein nursed her until her death in December 1945. Then, at the age of thirty-nine, Gein found himself alone in the world, deprived of the mother who had been his only contact with some kind of reality.

Perhaps the single thing which flawed Gein's mind was when as a child he witnessed his mother killing a pig, slitting its stomach open and ripping out the entrails with her bare hands. It had turned his mind: the images of a dominant woman, blood, poking about inside a body. All this and his mother's too close interest in him, which prevented her from ever showing him any love.

Although Gein exhibited traits of necrophilia, transvestism and voyeurism, the basis of the Robert Bloch novel, which was the Oedipus complex theme, was far too simplistic. Gein did not want to replace his mother. He simply got intense satisfaction from mutilating dead women. Perhaps it was a symbolic form of revenge on his cold and unloving mother. Both women he murdered had resembled his mother: middle-aged, overweight and dominant. Was he killing his mother over and over again? Certainly he did not worship her or her memory – she would never have allowed those pornographic magazines in the house, for example.

On Wednesday, 27 November, police dug up a rubbish pit on Gein's land and found the complete skeleton of a man with a gold tooth in the skull. It was one of the missing hunters, police surmised. However, forensic tests revealed that the skeleton was that of a woman. She was never identified.

In the mental hospital, Gein was again questioned and given lie-detector tests. Calmly he confessed to stealing nine corpses to take home and butcher. All had been middle-aged women.

On 18 December, the doctors at the hospital concluded that Gein was hopelessly insane and was not mentally competent to stand trial. Gein was brought before Judge Bunde on 6 January 1958. He sat in the dock, chewing gum while psychiatrists told the jude of their findings. After listening to their testimony, the judge committed Gein to the state mental hospital for an indefinite period. He would not stand trial for his crimes, although technically, should he ever regain his sanity, he could be tried.

The people of Plainfield protested bitterly at this result, and were even more enraged to learn that Gein's farm was to be sold at auction, with the proceeds presumably going to Gein or his estate. On the evening of 20 March, just prior to the auction, the people of Plainfield burned Gein's farmhouse to the ground. They wanted to destroy all traces of the charnel house which had stood in their midst and stained their town. The police did not look too hard for the mystery arsonist.

Gein proved to be a model inmate at the hospital, always helpful, getting on well with the staff and keen to pursue his hobbies. In January 1968, District Attorney Robert Gollmar received a letter from the hospital authorities informing him that Gein was now considered fit to stand trial. The trial took place the following November, the jury finding Gein both guilty, and not guilty by reason of insanity. The trial judge ordered Gein to be returned to the hospital and formally announced that the case was closed for all time.

In February 1974 Gein petitioned to be released, claiming that after sixteen years' incarceration he was now cured and sufficiently punished. The psychiatrists disagreed with Gein and he was kept in custody.

Gein died of respiratory failure on 26 July 1984, in the geriatric ward of the Mendota Mental Health Institute, where he had been cared for since 1978. He was seventy-seven years old. He was laid to rest in an unmarked grave in Plainfield Cemetery – right next to his mother.

The Gein case led to a spate of sick jokes in Wisconsin, known locally as 'Geiners'. Example: 'Why did Eddie keep the heating turned up in his house? So the furniture wouldn't get goose-bumps.' Childish, perhaps, but such grim humour was both valuable and necessary. It was cathartic, allowing the people in the community to come to terms with the unthinkable by means of laughter. Similar jokes were noted during the five-year hunt for the Yorkshire Ripper.

The Ripper hunt was said to have led to the premature death of George Oldfield, the senior officer in the inquiry. The same fate befell Sheriff Schley. He died in March 1960 of a heart attack shortly after testifying at Gein's trial. He was forty-three. Not all victims of a murderer are killed directly by him; some die from sheer stress, fright, or an excess of mourning. The relatives can be counted among the victims in this respect.

Ed Gein was a one-off, one of the few genuine monsters in the catalogue of murder; and in his case the sexual element in cannibalism can be clearly identified.

4
MAD, BAD, DEAN BAKER

At three o'clock on the afternoon of Saturday, 11 July 1970, a man out fishing on the banks of the Yellowstone River in Montana snagged a human body at the end of his line. He drove in shock to the nearest ranch to telephone the police, and Deputy Bigelow, who was stationed at the entrance to Yellowstone National Park responded to the call.

With the aid of some local men, the deputy waded into the turbulent river and dragged the body to shore. Although accustomed to routine drowning cases, Bigelow knew immediately that this was murder. The head was missing.

Bigelow called Sheriff Don Guitoni, who drove Coroner Davis to the scene. All three men crouched over the body, which was clad only in shorts. It was that of a male. Apart from the missing head, the arms had also been severed at the shoulders and the legs chopped off at the knees. The abdomen and chest were covered with stab wounds, with a particularly large ugly hole in the chest.

The coroner looked shocked when he concluded his examination. 'I never saw anything like it,' he said grimly. 'The poor fellow's been stabbed about twenty-five times and I figure he's been in the water about a day . . . He was a young fellow, probably in his early twenties.' He paused. 'There's one other thing,' he said. 'The heart is missing!' The chest had been cut open and the heart removed.

For the sheriff it was a major headache. All normal means of identifying the body – the head and hands – had been deliberately removed. But why the gratuitous butchery of the rest of the body? Why cut off the legs? Why remove the heart?

The only thing it suggested was that it was some form of cult murder. There had been a rash of them recently, all connected with secret groups of devil-worshippers. The Sharon Tate case had grabbed the headlines, but similar bizarre killings were going on all over the USA.

The torso was taken by ambulance to the morgue in Livingston for a proper autopsy to be carried out, while police teletyped details of the victim to Wyoming and other neighbouring states. It was impossible to tell where the body had been dumped in the river, and the Yellowstone passed through Wyoming before entering Montana and the National Park. Although police searched the river and its banks for many miles, no traces of the missing limbs were found.

The results of the autopsy indicated that the victim had been stabbed twenty-seven times with a sharp-pointed blade of at least five inches in length. The removal of the head and limbs had been crudely performed, possibly with the knife used to inflict the stab wounds. The victim was in his early twenties and had been dead for twenty-four hours when found. Police had to wait until someone was reported missing.

On the Monday morning a teletype message came chattering into the sheriff's office in Livingston, concerning a missing person who resembled the description of the torso. James Michael Schlosser, aged twenty-two, had been reported missing from the town of Roundup, a hundred miles away, that same morning.

He had set out on the Friday to drive to Yellowstone Park in his Opel Kadett sports car, but had not turned up for work on the Monday. When his office colleagues got in touch with his landlady, they discovered that the popular young social worker had not returned home.

160

Schlosser was described as being six feet tall and weighing two hundred pounds. The age, height and weight fitted the torso. Sheriff Guitoni put out an alert for sightings of his Opel Kadett car, which might have been dumped in the area. It was a 1969 vehicle, yellow, with black racing stripes.

An hour later that same car was in a collision with a pick-up truck on a dirt road in Monterey County, California, just a few miles from the Pacific Ocean. The car had been travelling at speed on the wrong side of the road. The truck suffered only a dented bumper, but the car was a write-off. The driver of the truck was a businessman from Detroit on holiday. He got out of his truck and approached the car, from which two large young men were emerging. Both men were typical Californian hippies, with long hair and beards.

One was blond, the other dark. The blond man was about six feet tall and very powerfully built, with shoulder-length golden hair. He wore a leather waistcoat and bell-bottom trousers, topped with an Army fatigue jacket. His companion wore cowboy boots and a green Army field jacket. The businessman might have expected trouble, but the hippies were friendly.

The businessman wanted to exchange driver's licences, but neither hippy had one, so he took the registration number of their vehicle and suggested he should drive them both to the nearest telephone so the police could be notified of the accident. Both hippies shrugged and got into his truck. But when he drove into a service station in the town of Lucia, both men got out and ran away into nearby woods.

The businessman phoned the police and told them about the incident, giving the registration number of the other vehicle. It was that of the car belonging to the missing Schlosser, and the California Highway Patrol were alerted to keep an eye out for two hippies, wanted in connection with a homicide.

Patrolman Randy Newton was out cruising the Pacific

Coast Highway when he got the call over his radio, and he turned off into a dirt side-road, figuring that the two fugitives could not have got far.

He came upon the suspects walking along the road just two miles out of Lucia, trying to hitch a lift. The two men had no identification, but readily admitted having been the two men in the Opel Kadett involved in the accident. Newton arrested both men and radioed for assistance. When fellow officers arrived, the two suspects were handcuffed and advised of their rights.

But the blond man seemed anxious to talk, positively eager, even. Identifying himself as Stanley Dean Baker, aged twenty-three, and his companion as Harry Allen Stroup, aged twenty, Baker said they were both from Sheridan, Wyoming, and had been travelling together since 5 June, hitching lifts when they could.

The prisoners were searched, and in Baker's pockets police found small lengths of bone. Officer Newton studied them curiously and asked Baker what they were.

Baker blurted out: 'They ain't chicken bones. They're human fingers.' Then he added, memorably and in typically American phraseology: 'I have a problem. I'm a cannibal.'

Both men were taken to the police station in Monterey, Baker continuing to talk in the patrol car about his compulsion to eat human flesh. He claimed to have developed a taste for it after having electric shock treatment for a nervous disorder when he was seventeen, and referred to himself as 'Jesus'.

At the police station Detective Dempsey Biley took over the questioning. Baker almost boasted of how he had killed the owner of the Opel Kadett, saying Stroup had not been with him at the time. He and Stroup had split up when they reached Big Timber, a few miles from Livingston, because Baker had managed to hitch a ride with James Schlosser.

When Schlosser had said he was going to the Yellowstone Park for the weekend, Baker had asked to go along, and the two men had set up camp for the night close to the Yellowstone River.

In the middle of the night Baker had crept over to his sleeping companion and shot him twice in the head with a .22 pistol he habitually carried. Then he had cut up the body into six parts, removing the head, arms and legs. When asked what he had done with the dead man's heart, Baker replied: 'I ate it. Raw.'

He explained that he had cut off the dead man's fingers to have something to chew on, and dumped the remainder of the body in the river, along with the pistol, before driving off in his victim's car.

Later he had met up with Harry Stroup along the road and offered him a lift. He insisted that Stroup had not been involved in the murder.

Both men were searched thoroughly and among Baker's possessions was a recipe for LSD and a paperback book called *The Satanic Bible*, which was a handbook of devil-worship with instructions on how to conduct a black mass.

Baker described the location of the camp where he had killed Schlosser, and when police officers located it and searched it, they found evidence that murder had indeed taken place at that spot. The earth was splattered with dried blood and a bloodstained hunting knife was found. There was also the usual debris which accompanies any such murder: human bone fragments, teeth, skin and a severed human ear.

The pair were taken before a judge in California and waived extradition. Subsequently they were flown back to Montana, where they were arraigned before District Judge Jack Shamstrom on 27 July. The pair were remanded in Park County jail, but on 4 August Judge Shamstrom approved a motion that Baker be sent to Warm Springs State Hospital for psychiatric evaluation. Harry Stroup had remained silent throughout, apparently guilty of nothing more than having befriended a homicidal maniac and devil-worshipper. Those short lengths of bone found on Baker were sent to a pathologist for examination and proved to be bones from a human right index finger.

No motive for the crime was claimed by the prosecution, apart from the cannibal aspect: the lust for human flesh. But as we have seen from an examination of man-eating tribes in New Guinea and elsewhere, the eating of a slain foe symbolizes total conquest and total contempt for the victim, who is digested and then excreted.

It may be that Baker, the non-conforming hippy with no job, viewed the young Schlosser, a college graduate with a sports car, horn-rimmed glasses and expensive camping equipment, as a respectable 'square' who had prospered within the system; a symbol of everything he could not be and a mirror to his own failure.

In that case envy would be the motive, a 'have-not' who saw himself as a social reject, lashing out violently at a respectable member of society – with the same blind ferocity as a snake striking at a stick.

5
KEMPER THE CANNIBAL

Murder is a subject statistically well-documented. In Britain the murder rate over the past twenty years has remained fairly constant, within a range of 3.6 to 5.0 per million of population. But in the United States there has been a virtual epidemic of murder ever since 1960. The American murder rate is twenty times higher than Britain's. One startling statistic will suffice to prove the point. From the period 1970 to 1974, more people were murdered in the USA than were killed during the entire Vietnam war.

Using statistics, it is possible to construct an Identikit profile of murder, murderers and victims. The typical murderer is male, aged twenty, and in sixty per cent of all cases he will know his victim. A quarter of all murders occur within the family. He will kill with a gun in two-thirds of all cases, with a knife in nineteen per cent, assault in eight per cent, drown in seven per cent, and burn, asphyxiate by gas or throw the victim from a high building in seven per cent.

In America you are much more likely to be killed in the home than anywhere else; the street is the next most popular site. Murder is much more likely to occur at weekends, by night rather than day, and is more frequent during holiday periods than any other.

When discussing murderers, it is important to distinguish between mass murderers and serial killers. The mass murderer kills a number of people in a single episode – a typical example is the killing of eight student nurses in Chicago in 1966 by Richard Speck. The serial killer murders a number of people in an episodic manner on separate occasions; for example, Peter Sutcliffe, the 'Yorkshire Ripper', murdered thirteen women during a five-year killing spree.

Time and again one has to turn to America to spot the coming trends in murder. For example, would it be feasible to expect two serial killers to be operating in the same small area? Possibly, but how about *three?* The odds against would seem to be astronomical, and yet that is precisely what happened in the relatively small area of Santa Cruz, California, during the period 1970 to 1973. A mass murderer killed in 1970, while two serial killers operated during 1972 to 1973, dumping victims on each other's sites and thus confusing the police investigation. Between them, John Frazier, Edmund Kemper and Herbert Mullins killed a total of twenty-six people, and for a couple of years Santa Cruz had the unenviable reputation of being the 'murder capital' of the world.

On 19 October 1970, John Linley Frazier killed eye surgeon Dr Victor M. Ohta, his wife, Virginia, their two young sons, Taggart and Derrick, eleven and twelve respectively, and Dr Ohta's secretary, Dorothy Cadwallader. Dr Ohta had been shot three times, the others once in the back of the head. The bodies were then thrown into the swimming-pool of the doctor's luxury home at Santa Cruz. The killer then set the house on fire.

When firemen arrived to deal with the blaze, they found the doctor's red Rolls-Royce blocking the drive. Under the windscreen wiper was a typewritten note which read: *Today World War III will begin, as brought to you by the people of the Free Universe. From this day forward any one and/or company of persons who misuses the natural environment or destroys the same will suffer the penalty of death by the people of the Free Universe. I and my comrades from this day forth will fight until death or freedom against anyone who does not support natural life on this planet. Materialism must stop or mankind will stop*. It was signed: *Knight of Wands – Knight of Pentacles – Knight of Cups – Knight of Swords*. The writer was obviously familiar with the Tarot pack.

The massacre caused panic in the area. Coupled with the strange note, the murders seemed to be the work of a Manson-type gang, and contingents of hippies lived in the local woods. However, police investigations revealed it to be the work of one man, John Frazier, a twenty-four-year-old drop-out mechanic from Santa Cruz, who lived in an old cowshed near the Ohta property and was separated from his wife.

Frazier had been exhibiting symptoms of mental illness for five months before the killings, after he had been involved in a car accident. He was uninjured, but told his wife he had heard God's voice saying: 'If you drive again you will be killed.' From this time on he became convinced that he was an agent of God's will, with a mission to save the world from materialism.

He became convinced that the Revelation of St John the Divine in the Bible was specifically addressed to him; that he had been reincarnated – he had been born in India ten generations previously – and had been sent back to earth to save it from destruction. He developed a bizarre philosophy based on the occult, astrology and numerology. His wife and mother begged him to have psychiatric treatment but he refused.

On Monday, 19 October, he carried out his divine mission. He was not hard to catch: neighbours reported their suspicions about him, and a check revealed that he had convictions for burglary. His fingerprints were found on the door of the Rolls-Royce, and on a beer-can found in the house. He refused to talk and remained silent throughout his trial. He was found guilty on five counts of murder and sentenced to death. He joined the long queue on death row in San Quentin.

Edmund Emil Kemper, born 18 December 1948, suffered severe psychological disturbance as a child. He cut the hand and feet off his sister's doll, and at thirteen cut the family cat into pieces. He had sadistic fantasies about killing his mother, whom he felt had rejected him. In fact, he had been brought up very strictly, with his mother often locking him in the cellar. Most killers of this type have a history of abuse as a child. His mother and father separated when he was seven; at thirteen Kemper ran away to his father, who promptly sent him back to his mother. He was then sent to live with his paternal grandparents on a ranch in California. On 27 August 1963 he shot and stabbed his grandparents to death in a fit of rage. Then he telephoned his mother to tell her what he had done, explaining: 'I just wondered how it would feel to shoot Grandma.'

The courts ordered him to be detained in a mental hospital, and after five years of treatment he was released in 1969 into the care of his mother. He was now twenty-one years of age, and tests had shown him to have an above-average intelligence, with an IQ of 136.

He had been examined in the hospital by psychiatrist Donald T. Lunde, who was to write about him in his book *Murder and Madness*.

In those intervening years between killing his grandparents and being released upon society, he had grown to be a freak: six feet nine inches tall, weighing twenty stone. Although he had a strong sexual drive, he had no hope of a normal relationship with a woman. Not unless he killed her . . .

As he was to say later: 'If I killed them, you know, they couldn't reject me as a man. It was more or less making a doll out of a human being . . . a carrying-out of my fantasies with a living human doll.'

He had been released as 'cured' and received no after-care treatment. Despite his high intelligence he took labouring jobs, and began collecting knives. His favourite, and the one he always used for killing, he called 'the General'. He began cruising the roads in his car, looking for girls to pick up.

Between 7 May 1972 and 21 April 1973, Kemper killed eight women by shooting, stabbing and strangulation. He cut limbs off the victims, attempted sexual relations with the corpses, and committed acts of cannibalism.

His first six victims were hitch-hikers. On 7 May he picked up Anita Luchese and Mary Ann Pesce, both students of eighteen at Fresno State College. He held a gun on the girls and made Anita climb into the trunk, while he handcuffed Mary Ann, putting a plastic bag over her head. He then stabbed her several times in the back, then in the abdomen, before cutting her throat. Then he killed the other girl. He took the bodies home – his mother was out – and dissected and decapitated them, having sex with the headless corpses. He took Polaroid photographs of the results of his handiwork, then buried the pieces on the mountains.

On 14 September he picked up fifteen-year-old Aiko Koo, killed her, raped her, then cut up her body. On 8 January 1973 he picked up Cynthia Schall, who was eighteen. This time he kept the body overnight in his bedroom closet, then next morning performed sexual acts on the body before dissecting it. He actually chopped the body up with an axe. On 5 February he picked up two victims, Rosalind Thorpe, twenty-three, and Alice Lui, twenty-one. He shot them both in the head, then decapitated them. He took the bodies home and had intercourse with them, leaving the heads in the trunk of his car.

By now parts of the missing girls had been found, and the newspapers were screaming about the 'Co-ed Killer' whom the police were actively hunting.

Kemper was something of a police groupie. He hung around with them, drinking in local bars and discussing the current brutal murders. But by now Kemper was totally out of control.

On Easter Sunday – 21 April 1973 – Kemper killed his mother and one of her friends, Sarah Hallett. He first struck his mother over the head with a hammer, then decapitated her with the General and cut out her larynx, putting it into the garbage disposal unit. He explained later: 'It seemed appropriate, as much as she'd bitched and screamed and yelled at me over all the years.' He killed Mrs Hallett later, when she arrived to visit his mother, saying she was 'dead on her feet'.

Kemper sexually attacked the headless body of his mother, and after he had glutted himself, he slept that night in his mother's bed. He was a treasure-trove for the Freudian analyst.

He had left a note behind at the death scene, assuming the police would find it. With more than a streak of black humour, it read: *Appx 5.15 a.m. Saturday. No need for her to suffer any more at the hands of this 'murderous Butcher'. It was quick – asleep – the way I wanted it. Not sloppy or incomplete, gents. Just a 'lack of time'. I got things to do!!!*

After a period on the run, expecting a manhunt and finding none, Kemper did something killers of his type rarely do. He realized that he could not stop himself killing – he was driven by a compulsion beyond his control – and so he gave himself up to the police. But it was not that easy. Kemper was afraid to walk into a police station, fearing violence from the police. So he telephoned to surrender himelf as being the Co-ed Killer, but the police dismissed it as a crank call. Kemper had to phone three times before he could get police to come and take him in.

He was questioned at length, readily admitted his crimes and, according to journalist Don West, he confessed to having eaten the flesh of two of his victims, explaining how he 'cut flesh from their legs, freezing it and then cooking it in a macaroni casserole'. Later, during further questioning, he revealed how he kept mementoes of his victims: their teeth, and pieces of their skin.

During his trial Kemper went into the witness box and was extremely articulate. Evidence had been given about his mental history, and Kemper told the court: 'I believe very deeply there are two people inside me.' Asked why he had eaten parts of his victims, Kemper replied: 'I wanted them to be part of me – and now they are.'

A court-appointed psychiatrist said that Kemper was 'very intelligent' and 'would kill again if given the opportunity'. The jury found him to be legally sane, and also found him guilty of the eight counts of first-degree murder he faced. Despite making a plea to be executed, Kemper had to accept a term of life imprisonment, and he too was sent to San Quentin.

At exactly the same period as Kemper was killing, Herbert Mullin was littering Santa Cruz with the bodies of thirteen people. His murders took place between 13 October 1972 and 13 February 1973.

Born on 18 April 1947, Mullin had an ordinary childhood with no signs of psychological disturbance. At seventeen a close friend, Dean, died, and this seemed to trigger off schizophrenia in Mullin. He made a shrine to Dean in his bedroom. In February 1969, when he was twenty-one, he announced that he was going to India to study religion. Then he began exhibiting bizarre symptoms: mimicking everything anyone said, and staring into space. He was persuaded to enter a mental hospital, but left after a few weeks. He began to drift, working as a dish-washer, then a gas-station attendant, while complaining to friends that he kept hearing voices. He wrote many letters to people he had never met, signing himself: *a human sacrifice, Herb Mullin.*

The 'voices' now became *command hallucinations* ordering him to do certain things, like shave his head or burn his penis with a lighted cigarette. He was admitted to a mental hospital as being 'a person who is a danger to others'. But a month later he was discharged, the doctors stating that 'the prognosis is very grave'.

He left home and lived in San Francisco for a year, cutting all contacts with his family. When he returned, his parents realized that they couldn't handle him and tried several times to get him committed, without success.

The voices were now urgent, saying: 'Herb, I want you to kill me somebody.' His writings at this time were full of references to Einstein, charts and prayers, biblical quotations and reincarnation. On 13 October 1972, while driving along a deserted highway in the Santa Cruz mountains, Mullin saw an old hobo, Lawrence White. He stopped the car, killed the old man with a baseball bat, and drove on. Eleven days later he picked up hitch-hiker Mary Guifoyle, stabbed her to death, and left her body in the mountains. On 2 November he stabbed a Catholic priest to death in the confessional.

On 16 December he bought a handgun. The voices were becoming more insistent. He must kill again. On 25 January he drove out to Branciforte Drive, looking for a man who years before had turned him on to pot: Jim Gianera. Mullin believed that Gianera had set out to destroy his mind. He went to Gianera's cabin, but he no longer lived there. The new tenant, Kathy Francis, gave him the new address. Mullin went there, shot Gianera dead, and stabbed his wife to death as she bent over her dying husband. He then returned to the cabin and killed twenty-nine-year-old Kathy and her two young sons.

On 6 February he was wandering around a state park in Santa Cruz when he saw a tent. Inside were four boys. Mullin told them he would have to report them for camping illegally, and when they protested, shot them all dead. A few days later, while delivering firewood to his parents' home, the voice said: 'Before you deliver the wood I want you to kill me somebody.' Driving through town he saw an old man, Fred Perez, working in his garden. He stopped the car, shot him dead, and then drove on. But neighbours had seen his station-wagon and were able to describe it to the police. Mullin was arrested before reaching his parents' house.

At his trial in the Santa Cruz County courthouse, Mullin tried to explain his motives to the baffled jury. 'I,

Herb Mullin, was chosen as the designated leader of my generation by Professor Albert Einstein on 18 April 1955.' He went on to say that natural catastrophes were averted only by human sacrifice. He had personally averted earthquakes in California by his killings – there hadn't been one, had there?

Both prosecution and defence were united in agreeing that Mullin had committed the killings for which he stood charged, and that he was seriously mentally ill. But the question at issue was whether he was *insane by legal standards*. It was to be a long trial.

During the course of it, a whimsical jailer had placed Mullin and Kemper in adjoining cells. They hated each other. Kemper referred to Mullin as 'a creep with no class', and was annoyed that Mullin had dumped victims in *his* area; for his part, Mullin hated Kemper as being 'a brutal, immoral animal'. His own murders had been for a *purpose*, not simply sexual gratification.

During his evidence, Mullin told the court that he had not been responsible for the decision to kill. 'A rock doesn't make a decision while it's falling. It just falls.' And after all, there *hadn't* been any earthquakes in California in 1973 . . .

The jury found him to be legally sane and guilty of the murders. He was sentenced to consecutive life sentences, with the result that he will not be eligible for parole until 2020, sometime after his seventy-third birthday.

After the trial, jury foreman Ken Springer wrote an open letter to the then State Governor Ronald Reagan. 'None of this need ever have happened . . . Five times prior to young Mr Mullin's arrest he was entered into mental hospitals. Five times his illness was diagnosed. Yet in January and February of this year he was free to take the lives of Santa Cruz residents . . . '

It was a plea to prevent Governor Reagan from closing any more mental hospitals, which he was doing as part of his tight budgetary control economy measures. The next year the legislature passed a bill to that effect, but the damage was done. Those closed were not reopened.

6
KROLL'S DEEP-FREEZE

In July 1959 the body of a sixteen-year-old girl, Manuela Knodt, was found near the village of Bredeney, south of Essen. She had been strangled and raped, and the autopsy revealed that she had been a virgin prior to her death.

The police of the Ruhr area of Germany were accustomed to dealing with sex-killings of this type – Germany has always had a high rate of sex-related offences – but what made this case unusual was a peculiar trade-mark of the killer: he had removed large slices of flesh from the buttocks and thighs of his victim.

The next murder in the series came on 23 April 1962, when thirteen-year-old Petra Giese, who had gone to visit a carnival at the village of Rees, near Walsum, failed to return home. The following day her body was found in a forest a mile from the village. Her red dress had been ripped from her body in a frenzy, and she had been strangled and raped. This time both buttocks and the left forearm had been removed and taken away. There was only one possible motive for these mutilations that the police could come up with: the killer had taken them home to *eat*.

Two months later, on 4 June, another girl, Monika Tafel, suffered the same fate. She was on her way to school in Walsum when she was attacked and dragged into a field to be strangled and raped. Again, the killer had cut steaks from her buttocks and the inside of her thighs. It was a trade-mark the police were becoming all too familiar with.

By now the press had begun calling the unknown killer the Ruhr Hunter. He struck again on 22 December 1966, when he strangled five-year-old Ilona Harke in a park near Wuppertal, raped her, then removed steaks from her buttocks and shoulders.

It was ten years before the police heard from the Ruhr Hunter again. Four-year-old Marion Ketter was playing with friends in a playground in the Duisburg suburb of Laar. It was a hot day and she was dressed only in knickers – a fact which might have prompted the killer to attack – when a mild-looking man with a bald head was seen speaking to the child, then leading her away.

Her mother missed her minutes later, and rushed to the police. As a result, a large detachment of police moved into the area and began making door-to-door inquiries. In one apartment block an elderly tenant told them something interesting. His neighbour, a man named Joachim Kroll, who worked as a lavatory attendant, had advised him not to use the lavatory on the top floor of the building because it was blocked up. When the tenant asked: 'With what?' Kroll had replied bluntly: 'With guts.' It may have been just a sick joke . . .

A plumber was called to examine the toilet. It was indeed blocked with guts – the internal organs and entrails of a small child.

Police raided Kroll's flat and discovered parcels of human flesh neatly wrapped in plastic bags in the deep-freeze – and, even more horrifying, in the bubbling sauce-pan on the stove they found a child's hand among the carrots and potatoes.

Kroll was a slight, elderly man, with meek brown eyes, and when questioned it became immediately apparent that he was mentally subnormal. When he was taken to the police station, he asked officers to quickly give him the operation to make him harmless to women so that he could return home for his dinner.

Police questioned Kroll in depth and discovered that he had committed far more than the five cannibal murders they had attributed to him. Although his memory was poor – he apologized for this fact – Kroll could recall his first criminal attacks on women, and typically, he had begun as a rapist before graduating to murder.

His first rape-murder had been committed in February 1955, near the village of Walstedde. Irmgard Strehl, an attractive blond girl of nineteen, was found in a barn, strangled. She had been raped. The lack of bruising to her genitals indicated that she had not resisted the rape, nor were there any typical defensive wounds.

On 17 June 1959 Klara Tesmer was found in woods near Rheinhausen. She too had been strangled, stripped and raped. There was nothing to link the two murders.

Kroll told the detectives all about his career of rape-murder, almost innocently, like a child talking about the toys with which he plays. He lived alone, and in his flat he had electric gadgets and sex-aids, including several inflatable rubber dolls. He often strangled one of these with one hand while masturbating with the other.

He resembled the English sex-killer Christie, who was too nervous and timid to have sex with a conscious and mature woman. They had to be *dead*. So at the age of twenty-two Kroll had begun satisfying his sexual urges with acts of rape. He had devoted most of his life to this pursuit, wandering around for hours at a time looking for girls on their own he could attack. He had lost count of his murders, and although he could remember a dozen in some detail, there were obviously many more.

Examples included an attempted attack on 22 August 1965, when Kroll was hiding near Grossenbaum, watching a couple having sex in a parked car. He became so excited that he determined to rape the girl. But it ended in fiasco when he was forced to stab her lover to death and flee the scene.

A year later, on 13 September 1966, he killed and raped Ursula Roling, who left the apartment she shared with her boyfriend to visit her parents in Marl. She never arrived. Her body was discovered two days later, hidden in bushes, naked from the waist down and with her legs spread wide apart.

The boyfriend was taken in and questioned for three days, despite his plea that since he lived with the victim, he had no need to rape her. What had aroused police suspicions was that the victim displayed no sign of bruising, or of having resisted the rape. (The dead do not bruise, of course.) The boyfriend was eventually released but it took Kroll's confession ten years later to finally clear his name.

The reason why Kroll had been able to murder undetected for a period of over twenty years was that he killed over such a wide area that the police had no reason to link the deaths as being the work of one man. Kroll was simply one among many sex-killers operating in this period.

He did come close to being caught in 1976, when he was living in the small town of Grafenhausen. He enticed a ten-year-old girl to go into a meadow with him to look at a rabbit, then produced a magazine of pornographic photographs and showed them to her. With his limited intelligence, Kroll had assumed that they would excite her as they had him. The girl was horrified and fled. Kroll left the town the same day, and the girl never reported the incident to her parents.

On 12 July 1969 Maria Heetgen, a sixty-one-year-old widow, answered a knock at the door of her flat in Hueckeswagen and was immediately strangled by the man at the door, who dragged her lifeless body into the hall and stripped and raped her before leaving. The crime was never connected with the Ruhr Hunter.

On 21 May 1970, Jutta Rahn, aged thirteen, walked from her home to catch the train to her school in Essen. She had to pass through woods for part of the way. She was strangled and raped by Kroll. A local man was arrested for the crime and remained under suspicion until Kroll's final confession.

In 1976 Karin Toepfer, aged ten, was strangled and raped while on her way to school in Dinslaken Voerde, and once again the police had no reason to link the crime to those of the Ruhr Hunter, because the trade-mark of the missing flesh was absent.

Kroll told the police that unlike Fish, his cannibalism was not sexually motivated. He simply felt that he might as well save money on buying meat by taking steaks from his victims, providing they were suitably tender.

The police knew that there must have been other murders. It seemed unlikely that Kroll had waited from 1955 until 1959 before committing his second sex-murder. What had taken place in the intervening years?

Kroll's memory was prodded, and he remembered murdering and raping twelve-year-old Erika Schuleter in the town of Kirchhellen in 1956, and the murder of another twelve-year-old girl, Barbara Bruder, whom he had killed in 1962. Although this brought the total of known murders to fourteen, it is certain that there were many more.

With simple animal cunning, Kroll was able to kill and outwit the police for over twenty years.

7

A CANNIBAL IN PARIS

Renee Hartwelt was a twenty-five-year-old Dutch girl studying at the Censier Institute in Paris. A very bright student, she had gained a degree from the University of Leyden and came to Paris at the beginning of 1981 to do post-graduate work in French literature for her PhD.

She was big, blond and pretty, but there was nothing frivolous about her. She was single-minded in her determination to succeed on her own terms. This daughter of a retired industrialist was very serious by nature, a hard-working student who never missed a lecture, spoke fluent French and German, and could converse easily in English. She refused to accept any money from her wealthy family and suported herself by giving private lessons in French and German. She lived rent-free in a maid's room in an apartment building at 59 Rue Bonaparte, in exchange for looking after the two children of the landlord. In this manner she covered all her expenses without recourse to family help or even a grant.

When she failed to appear for lectures on Friday, 12 June 1981, her friends and fellow students were both surprised and concerned. Some of them went to the Rue Bonaparte later that day to inquire about her well-being, fearing that she might be ill. Although it was an exceptionally hot day, Renee was not the kind of girl to miss lectures simply because it was sunny.

The landlord said he had not seen Renee at all that day, and she was not in her room. He was persuaded to use his pass key to enter her room; everything was in order, with the bed neatly made, and only the occupant missing.

Saturday, 13 June passed, and there was still no sign of Renee. The landlord had to look after his own children, and was concerned enough to go to the police to report Renee missing. He was told that since she was an adult, she had no need to account to anyone for her movements. However, if she failed to turn up on Monday then the landlord should call back and the girl would be reported officially missing.

It was noon on the Saturday when the landlord went to the police station. Eight hours later, diners at a restaurant in the Bois de Boulogne noticed a tiny Asian man hurrying past with two large suitcases in the park outside the windows. Since he was less than five feet in height and weighed no more than six stones, the suitcases were actually heavier than he was. He was dragging them along on the small wheeled trolleys favoured by tourists, but even so, he was puffing and panting, red in the face from exertion. It was an odd – almost surrealistic – sight, even to blasé Parisians.

Forty-five minutes later the man appeared to tire of his task, because two girls walking in the Bois de Boulogne spotted him trying to push the suitcases into the lake. When he saw the girls he fled through the bushes like a startled cat, abandoning his luggage.

The girls were curious. They walked over to the suitcases and saw that one of them was heavily smeared with blood. That was enough to send them hurrying to phone the police. A police car soon arrived on the scene and radioed for detectives to be sent out. The girls gave a description of the man. The circumstances appeared to be very suspicious indeed.

A team of detectives, headed by an inspector, appeared. The inspector donned a pair of rubber gloves and gingerly opened the suitcases. Inside were ordinary plastic bags of the kind used to hold garbage. Intrigued, the inspector slit the bags open with a knife, spreading them apart to get a look at the contents. It was an action he was to regret instantly, since he nearly lost his lunch. Inside the bag he had cut open was a woman's face with the tip of the nose sliced off. The area was immediately cordoned off, awaiting the arrival of forensic experts.

The two girls who had spotted the man had been kept at the scene as witnesses to a potential homicide, and had to describe him over and over again. Witnesses were found from the restaurant who had also seen him wrestling with the suitcases. The descriptions were remarkably consistent.

Police cars raced around the roads in the hope of catching sight of the diminutive suspect, but since the Bois de Boulogne is a very large park with many paths, he could have lost himself at any point.

The suitcases, meanwhile, were taken to the police morgue, where a pathologist opened them. He found they contained most of the remains of a young woman. However, the lips, breasts and large chunks of the thighs and buttocks were missing. The head had been cut off, and the torso cut up into chunks small enough to fit into the suitcases. All the internal organs, including the intestines, were present. Also found in the suitcases were items of clothing which had presumably belonged to the dismembered woman: a summer dress, brassiere, white nylon panties, and socks and shoes. But there was nothing to identify the body, no purse or papers.

The post-mortem revealed that the victim had been killed with a .22 bullet fired from a rifle at point-blank range into the base of her skull. The bullet was recovered. She had been a large, blond girl in her mid-twenties, and had been dead for some forty-eight hours. There were semen traces in the vagina, indicating intercourse or rape shortly before death.

The dismembering of the body had been carried out crudely, with the sole object of making each part small enough to fit the suitcase – hence the removal of the head. But what was strange was that while the killer might have been expected to remove those parts of the body which could identify the victim – and thus himself – such as the head and hands, these had been left. What had been taken away made no sense. Only the fleshy soft parts had been removed. The sort of cuts a butcher might choose . . .

'You mean she was cut up for the cooking pot?' the inspector asked incredulously.

The pathologist nodded. 'That's what my examination leads me to believe,' he said. 'This is a big city, full of all kinds of people, many of them with serious mental problems. I am not suggesting that this is a cannibal in the sense of a savage who hunts women for food. But the body was cut up carefully and methodically with a razor-sharp knife. It wasn't the work of someone trained in anatomy – a doctor, say. It is, however, something which has been done by an intelligent, thinking person, one who went about things in a logical manner.'

The detectives were now faced with the task of tracing the Asian and identifying the dead woman. The second problem was the easier of the two, since the missing person's report on Renee Hartwelt was already in the police computer, and her description – large, blond, in her mid-twenties – was a perfect match for what lay on the slab in the police morgue.

On Monday, 15 June, the landlord and students from the university were asked to visit the police morgue to make a formal identification of the body. They were shown the head only, with the tip of the nose replaced. The identification was immediate. It was Renee Hartwelt. A technician took prints from the corpse and matched them with prints from possessions in her room, just to confirm the fact, and the dead girl's parents in Holland were notified of her gruesome death.

Even in Paris, a short Asian should not be hard to trace. The police had a good description of him, and witnesses were traced in a painstaking investigation which relied heavily on good old-fashioned foot-slogging.

Since the girl had been murdered on the afternoon of 11 June, the man's movements since that time were of critical importance.

One witness had seen him arrive in the Bois de Boulogne in a dark blue Peugeot 504 taxi, along with his embarrassing suitcases. It was only a matter of tracing every Peugeot taxi operating in the area on the day in question, and soon the police were interviewing the driver. He remembered his strange fare very well indeed. The man had spoken terrible French, and the suitcases had been so heavy that the driver had had to help him lift them in and out of the boot. The driver had picked up the man in the Rue Erlanger, but could not remember the number of the house. Driven there in a police car, he identified the building as being No. 10.

Rue Bonaparte is a long street running from St-Germain-des-Prés to the Jardin du Luxembourg on the Left Bank. On the opposite side of the river, in the sixteenth *arrondissement*, is Auteuil, and the short street lined with trees known as the Rue Erlanger. Renee Hartwelt had made her last journey along this route.

Her parents reported that Renee had written to them about a new friendship with a brilliant Japanese student, but hadn't given his name or height in her letter. There was no way of knowing whether he was very short.

The Rue Erlanger was quickly sealed off by the police, the concierge at No. 10 confirming that there was indeed an Asian living there in a studio attic apartment. In fact, on Friday, 12 June, he had rented a carpet shampoo machine from the Auteuil supermarket and had appeared to be very busy cleaning.

Police armed with rifles and wearing bullet-proof vests raced up the stairs of the apartment block and burst into the flat occupied by Issei Sagawa. The guns were carried because of a natural fear that a man who could eat a woman might have an even worse fate in store for a man.

Thirty-three-year-old Sagawa greeted the officers calmly. He had a genius-level IQ and had gained a master's degree from the University of Osaka, where he had written his thesis on the works of Shakespeare. He had been in France since April 1977 and was studying for a doctorate on the subject of the influence of Japanese literature on contemporary French writers. However, his French was execrable.

He did not – and could not – deny the murder of Renee Hartwelt. The .22 rifle which had killed her was leaning against a wall – ballistic tests later confirmed it as the murder weapon. Asked why he had the rifle, Sagawa explained that he had bought it when he first arrived in Paris, having been warned that many murderers lived there. It was for self-protection.

The inspector and his men were busy searching the apartment, when the refrigerator door was opened, and there resting on a shelf were one of the dead girl's lips, her left breast, and both buttocks. Asked what he had done with the rest – the other breast and lip and the flesh from the thighs – Sagawa calmly replied that he had eaten it.

'Cooked?' the inspector asked, barely able to get the words out.

Sagawa looked affronted. 'No, sliced thin and raw,' he said. He spoke with a gentle, lisping voice.

He said that he had met Renee Hartwelt at the university, where they attended the same lectures. He had twice visited her in her room to take tea and discuss literature. Then he had asked her to visit him in his room on the afternoon of Thursday, 11 June. Renee had duly arrived and they had tea and discussed literature. She offered to give Sagawa free lessons in French, since he spoke the language so poorly.

At this point Sagawa asked Renee to have sex with him, using an obscene French expression – the slang term commonly used in the gutter – probably because he didn't know the polite term. Renee was shocked and rejected his proposal, emphasizing that they were friends, and that was all.

185

They had been kneeling on the floor facing one another in the Japanese custom. Sagawa got to his feet, bowing politely, and seemed to accept the rejection in good part. Taking down a book of poetry by Schiller, he asked Renee to read it aloud to him, which she did. Sagawa approached her from behind and fired a single shot from his rifle into the back of her skull. The poetry reading ended abruptly.

Sagawa now undressed the blonde girl carefully, and when she was completely naked he had sex with the still-warm corpse. Then he fetched a straight razor and a knife, using them to cut off the tip of the nose and part of one of the breasts, which he then ate greedily. Raw.

His appetite temporarily glutted, he butchered the girl carefully, taking his time, and stowing each piece he wanted to keep in the refrigerator, dismembering the rest into pieces small enough to fit into the plastic garbage bags. While dismembering the bodies, Sagawa stopped from time to time to carefully photograph each stage of the process, as if anxious to keep a permanent record of his handiwork. The undeveloped film was later found in his studio.

His task completed, he ate a little more of his victim's flesh before going to bed to sleep soundly that night.

The following morning he went out to buy the suitcases, complete with small wheeled caddies, and rent the machine for shampooing carpets. There was quite a lot of blood to remove, and despite his care, forensic scientists were able to find traces later.

Sagawa told detectives that he had made three attempts to dispose of the incriminating suitcases, but each time he had been foiled in his attempt. There were too many people walking about in the Bois de Boulogne. Finally he tried to dispose of the remains of Renee Hartwelt in the lake – only to be spotted by the two girls.

Sagawa was placed in a special prison unit for psychiatric examination. He told warders that he was profoundly sorry for the distress he had caused to his parents and the girl's parents, and was deeply ashamed of the disgrace he had brought on his country. But for the victim he expressed no regret at all.

The psychiatrists interviewed him with the fixed notion that the big blond girl had presented a challenge to him, and her rejection had come as a blow to his pride and virility.

Sagawa poured scorn on the notion. He had not felt rejected. And while he had found Renee sexually attractive, that had not been the motive for the murder. He had had sex with her corpse simply because it was available and it would have been a pity to let it go to waste.

The real reason for the murder of Renee Hartwelt was that he wanted to eat her flesh. Ever since early youth he had dreamed of eating a young girl. Now he had accomplished this, and he had found the experience as deeply satisfying as he had hoped. The psychiatrists gave up in despair. Sagawa could not be persuaded to plead insanity. He thought his action quite sensible.

On 13 July 1982 Sagawa appeared in court, where the judge found him mentally incompetent to stand trial and ordered him to be confined in a secure mental hospital for an indefinite period. A Japanese author got in touch with Sagawa and eventually they collaborated on a bestseller about his case, *In the Fog*, and there are plans to make a film of the book, which details Sagawa's predilection for human flesh.

In the Fog has sold 200,000 copies and one review in a Tokyo newspaper called it 'beautifully done, outstanding among recent Japanese literature.' The blurb on the front cover of the book calls it: 'A shocking personal account of extreme behaviour,' and has a quote from Sagawa saying: 'Renee . . . was the most delicious meat I ever had.'

The first few chapters of the book recount Sagawa's growing infatuation with Renee, describing in detail her 'nice breasts, slender build, long white neck, transparent white skin, beautiful and gorgeous face . . . '

The next forty pages describe in gruesome detail how he first tried to eat her corpse with his teeth and how he stored various parts of her body in his refrigerator, to be cooked and eaten later. Sagawa, incidentally, told author Colin Wilson, who was on a lecture tour of Japan, that he was seeking an English publisher for his book.

In May 1984 Sagawa was transferred to a mental hospital in Japan, following pleas from his wealthy family in Yokohama. He was released in September 1985, when the doctors pronounced him 'cured'.

In February 1986, Sagawa was living in a bachelor flat in a town near Tokyo, busy writing a sequel to the best-selling *In the Fog*. He was under no kind of supervision. His release caused a storm of indignation in France. 'However can someone who committed a murder leave hospital and not have to answer for his crime?' a magazine demanded.

Under Japanese law, a Japanese national may be charged in Japan for crimes committed abroad, but the Justice Ministry announced that it had no plans to prosecute Sagawa. France refused to send Sagawa's dossier to Japan, and Paris regarded the case as closed. Japanese official sources said the lack of concern might be due to the fact that the victim was Dutch. France was anxious not to have the case become an embarrassment and ruin lucrative trade relations with Tokyo.

The latest news about Sagawa came in October 1989, when it was revealed that the man who killed and ate a girl eight years earlier was planning to open a vegetarian restaurant in Tokyo. Crime certainly paid for this cannibal . . .

Sagawa had become an established media figure, Japan's most infamous celebrity. Even his crime was parodied by the Rolling Stones with their recording: 'Too Much Blood'. But Sagawa had not finished. In March 1992 he was again in the news when it was reported that he was visiting Germany to take part in a TV programme from Hamburg's Premiere TV, talking about how he killed and ate his girlfriend. Also due to take part in the programme – watched live by millions of viewers – would be an interview with the brother of Renee Hartwelt, and with Japanese and French psychiatrists.

Sagawa's trip to Germany is the first time he has left Japan since his deportation from France, and has caused outrage among various factions. An official of the Netherlands embassy in Tokyo expressed shock and disbelief at Sagawa's trip and at the decision of the Japanese to grant him a passport. He said he would inform his government and considered the whole affair to be 'sick'.

The trip has also caused concern among doctors, who believe their former patient is still potentially dangerous. Dr Tsuguo Kaneko, Superintendent of Matsuawa Hospital where Sagawa was in care from 1984 to 1985, describes Sagawa as a psychopath and believes he should be prosecuted. 'Maybe he is a danger to foreign females,' the doctor said. 'He must be in prison. He committed murder and bears criminal responsibility.'

But the Japanese government considers Sagawa to be innocent of any crime, and sane enough to travel abroad. 'We checked beforehand with a doctor who said he was sane,' said the Deputy Director of the Foreign Ministry passport division.

A clue to Sagawa's apparent 'sanity' may lie in the insight into his character afforded by an old friend of his. She says she is afraid of what may happen to Sagawa when the media loses its fascination with him. 'It's like a protective wall for him,' she says. What might happen when that wall is removed? Will Sagawa kill again to attract further media scandal, to preserve his celebrity status?

8
ANNA ATE HER LOVER

Mönchen-Gladbach, a city with a population of over a quarter of a million, lies to the west of the Ruhr, close to the Dutch border. British troops are stationed there, and there is a flourishing vice industry. For those who seek such pleasures, porno shops, sex cinemas and brothels abound. The German police are hard-pressed to maintain order in certain districts of the city for this reason.

Sometime in June 1981 a barber disappeared from the city. Josef Wirtz, aged thirty-four, was not married and had no relatives to miss him, and his disappearance hardly caused a ripple. It certainly did not interest the police. He was just another missing person – and, in any case, he might well have decided to move on elsewhere.

He last worked at the barber's shop where he was employed on Saturday, 2 June. When he failed to turn up on the Monday, his boss shrugged his shoulders. Wirtz had little wages to come and had probably found a better job elsewhere, he reasoned. But if bosses do not care about missing workers, landlords do care about missing rent. Wirtz was to have paid the rent for his apartment on the Friday, but had not done so. When he did not return after work on the Monday, the landlord let himself into his flat to see if Wirtz had skipped without paying.

Apparently he had not. His personal possessions were still littered around the flat, as was all his clothing. Reassured, the landlord decided to wait. However, when Wirtz still had not come back after three days, the landlord called the barber's shop, only to be told that Wirtz had not turned up for work and was considered to have left his job. It was then that the landlord informed the police about his vanishing lodger. He was anxious to let the flat to someone else, but had to go through the formalities first.

The police sent over two officers to witness the landlord packing up Wirtz's belongings in a carton, which they then sealed with an official police seal. An inventory had been drawn up, with the police keeping one copy and the landlord another. If Wirtz failed to reclaim his goods within one year, the landlord was at liberty to sell them. The carton was stored in the basement.

In due course a detective arrived to take a missing-person statement from Wirtz's employer. He could tell the police little. Wirtz had been an indifferent barber, a tall man, handsome, with a neat black moustache, and wavy black hair which he wore to shoulder level. As to his whereabouts, he had probably wandered off to another city.

The police had recovered photographs of Wirtz from his apartment and circulated them with a request for information to all police stations in the nation. Although it was a routine missing-person request, the police thought the circumstances suspicious, since Wirtz had failed to take with him even his toothbrush. He had left his personal papers behind, and even a well-stocked fridge. It didn't make sense . . .

A month later, on Saturday, 7 July, a twenty-year-old woman called Christa Augsburg went for a walk in the Bunter Garten, a park to the north of the city. Wandering through the bushes of the ornamental garden, she stubbed her toe on a human skull, to which rotting flesh still adhered . . . She screamed loudly.

Detectives arriving at the scene had first to establish whether the human remains had been dumped there or had lain buried for some time. The police pathologist was able to establish that the skull had been exposed to the elements for about forty-eight hours – the presence of insects proved that – but that the man had been dead for some time prior to that. Cause of death pointed to murder.

The remainder of the skeletal bones were in plastic sacks, indicating that the murder had taken place elsewhere and the body dumped where it was found. After the necessary photographs had been taken, the remains were taken to the police morgue, where detailed examination led to a very precise report.

The bones were those of a man six feet one inch tall, weighing between one hundred and eighty and one hundred and eighty-five pounds, aged between thirty-two and thirty-seven, with long dark wavy hair worn shoulder length. The missing Wirtz had been found – his dental records established that. The man had been dead for about a month, and it appeared that at some time or another his head and body parts had been kept in a fridge.

What really worried detectives was the final conclusion in the report. The flesh had been trimmed from the larger bones of the body with a sharp knife, much as a butcher would cut up an animal carcass. Some bones had been cut in half with a circular saw and, significantly, so little flesh remained on these bones that there was not enough to make soup . . .

The police accepted the possibility of cannibalism from the start. The victim had either been murdered to stock someone's larder, or else a third party had happened on the body and cut it up for the pot. After identification by the dentist who had carried out extensive dental work on Wirtz, the belongings from his apartment were taken in their carton to join the body in the morgue. Somewhere in that jumble lay the clue to the killer.

The plastic bags which had contained parts of the body came in for close scrutiny. There were four of them. Two were untraceable, being typical supermarket bags, but two bore the logo of a shop which rented out video films.

That shop was visited, particular attention being paid to the horror films in stock. Whoever had cut up a human body would be likely to favour 'splatter' movies.

The records of all customers were on computer, together with addresses, and one named jumped out at detectives. Walter Krone was a twenty-nine-year-old ex-convict with a history of cannibalism. He had been jailed for seven years in 1980 for eating parts of a young girl who had been killed in a street accident. When his home was searched it was found to contain a large library on the subject of cannibalism, although Krone proved to be a reluctant cannibal, ashamed of his unnatural urges and desperate to be cured.

Krone turned out to be a red herring. When interviewed by detectives, he stubbornly insisted that he had given up being a cannibal, and prison psychologists who had had him under observation confirmed this. They had approved his release from jail after he had served only three and a half years of his sentence. The police kept the huge bearded man in custody as a suspect and went back to basics.

Wirtz must have been killed between 2 June – the last time he was ever seen alive – and 4 June, when he failed to report for work. He had not been killed and cut up in his apartment: forensic tests proved that. Nor had he ever been known to buy or possess a power saw. Detectives continued to interview every customer of the video shop who had ever rented horror films. It was a long and time-consuming business, turning up many weird customers but no suspects.

Then on 26 July detectives arrived at the fourth-floor apartment of Anna Martina Zimmermann, aged twenty-six, mother of two small children aged six and four. The apartment overlooked the main city railway station. It was just another routine door-to-door inquiry. Explaining that she was separated from her husband, Wilhelm Zimmermann, Frau Zimmermann ushered the detectives into her lounge.

They noted immediately her penchant for the macabre. Huge spiders roamed free in the apartment, as did snakes. Cages contained lizards and rats. On the kitchen table lay the bloody remains of Frau Zimmermann's pets. She had slaughtered them to provide meat for her children. Experienced policemen are only too aware that horror fans tend to live out their fantasies in their furnishings.

The apartment contained a bookcase crammed with video cassettes of horror movies, with large, garish posters on the walls. Frau Zimmermann freely admitted her interest in the grotesque but denied ever knowing anyone called Josef Wirtz. However, she gave herself away, referring to the man as a barber when his occupation had not been mentioned. That earned her a trip to police headquarters for more intensive questioning.

The inspector in charge of the case sent detectives to question every occupant of her apartment block in case Wirtz had been seen entering or leaving her flat, and other detectives were ordered to locate the husband, Wilhelm Zimmermann.

At the same time a detachment of forensic experts from the police laboratory arrived at the Zimmermann's flat to carry out tests, armed with a warrant for that purpose. Having removed all the pets, they began searching the apartment. An inspection of the deep-freeze revealed numerous plastic containers filled with what appeared to be human flesh . . .

The questioning of Frau Zimmermann took on a new and more urgent tone. She demanded to see a lawyer, and was actually talking to one in the detention cells when the reports of human flesh being found in her deep-freeze came through. Although tests would have to be carried out on the flesh to determine whether it was animal or human, there was no disguising a human finger, an ear, and a male sex organ found in one of those plastic containers.

Meanwhile Wilhelm Zimmermann had been located and brought to police headquarters. Told that parts of a human body had been found in his wife's freezer, he began to talk. He admitted having been an accessory to the murder of Wirtz but denied having killed him. It was Anna who had done the deed.

He said that Wirtz had been his wife's lover for two years; the affair had begun when he was still living with his wife. He had not objected to the liaison and had even encouraged it. His wife's sexual appetite was so voracious that he alone could not satisfy her, and he welcomed help.

He did not know why Anna decided to kill Wirtz, but suspected that he had proved to be sexually inadequate. She asked her husband to get her a power tool to cut up a body, and he supplied her with a large electric circular handsaw. Then he sat nervously in the lounge, among the spiders and snakes, while his wife plied Wirtz with liquor, into which she had stirred powerful sleeping tablets.

After a time Wirtz went into a sort of paralysis. Although not unconscious, he was powerless to resist Anna's efforts. She attempted to strangle him to death manually, but when this proved unsuccessful, she dragged him into the bathroom and drowned him in the bath, holding his head underwater until all air bubbles stopped.

Following the murder, with her children in the next room, Anna began to act out one of her horror video films. Laying Wirtz's body out on the long wooden table in the kitchen, she cut his body up into handy saucepan-size pieces, using the electric saw to cut through the bones where necessary. She had worked hard to create a pile of chops, roasts and steaks, packing the meat into fifty plastic containers. She intended drawing on this free meat supply at will, thereby saving on her butcher's bills . . .

It was only after a month, when she had already consumed much of the body, that she decided to get rid of the head and other large bones, as she needed the space in her freezer. She had dumped the unwanted parts of her former lover at the beginning of July, Zimmermann said.

Confronted with her husband's confession, Frau Zimmermann too confessed the truth of the affair, confirming the details of the killing and butchering. She was indicted for premeditated murder and was placed under observation in prison to determine whether whe was competent to stand trial. Her husband was also remanded in custody for observation, before being dealt with on the accessory charge.

Only a thrifty housewife, one suspects, would find such a utilitarian use for an unwanted lover . . .

9

GARY HEIDNIK: THE MAN WHO COLLECTED WOMEN

I make no apology for devoting so much space to Gary Heidnik; his is a case which demands study in depth, since it contains so many clues about what drives the modern cannibal. In this respect he is almost an archetypal figure.

Put simply, what drives the serial killer and the cannibal is the will-to-power identified by Adler. Some people desire inordinate power over others. If channelled negatively this can lead to the mass murderer and sexual criminal. The FBI have been tracking serial killers in the United States from their Behavioural Science Unit, based at the National Centre for the Analysis of Violent Crime at Quantico, Virginia, for more than a decade. The head of the NVAVC Squad is currently forty-five-year old John Douglas. The system operated by the FBI consists of putting on computer all the details of a crime, in the belief that behaviour reflects personality. From the clues the killer leaves behind, the FBI 'mind-hunters' can build up a profile of the killer – and usually they are remarkably accurate. Psychological profiling was first used in Britain in 1987 to trap Duffy, the Railway Murderer.

Describing how he puts himself into the mind of the killer, Douglas explains that sex murders are not committed for sexual gratification but to serve power needs. 'What they really want is to control the victim for a period of time, manipulate, dominate, have overall control for hours, if not days. They want to see the fear come across the victim's eyes, they want to hear them begging for their life. That's the turn-on.'

Power is the ultimate aphrodisiac, as Henry Kissinger said. A report in the *Guardian* dated 10 June, 1991 quotes from a book on the Craig and Bentley case by John Parris, the barrister who defended Craig. In the book, *Scapegoat*, Parris claims that the late Lord Goddard, who sentenced Bentley to hang, was a bloodthirsty bigot who gained a perverse pleasure from sentencing young men to be flogged or hanged.

'His clerk, Arthur Smith, told me he used to take a spare pair of striped trousers round for Goddard because he knew that Goddard always had an ejaculation when sentencing youths to be flogged or hanged', writes Mr Parris. In other words, just as we see the psychopath indulging in power trips in his crimes, so we have defenders of the law motivated by a craving for power.

It could be argued, in sociological terms, that the man in the street, feeling powerless, takes vicarious delight in reading about those who wield the ultimate power of life and death – hence the success of films like *Rambo* or the *Friday the Thirteenth* series. But the astonishing success of films like *The Silence of the Lambs* and novels like *American Psycho* must give us pause.

The public have demonstrated an almost insatiable desire to learn more about the phenomenon of the serial killer, and it is a comment on human nature that we make celebrities of such people. Because in making them celebrities – i.e., unlike normal people – we miss out an important truth: they are so *ordinary* and yet such sad people.

Before studying the case of Heidnik in detail, it might be instructive to examine something of the new genre. *The Silence of the Lambs* was based on the fine novel by Thomas Harris and features the work of the FBI's Behavioural Science Unit in Virginia. (It is the first time that the FBI have allowed film-makers access to the Unit.) The FBI were the first police force to study the serial killer, and in fact the very term 'serial killer' was coined in the seventies by FBI agent Robert Ressler, who chose the name because such killers, operating in an episodic nature, reminded him of the film serials he had watched as a child.

Ed Gein, the grisly psychotic killer of 1957, had formed the basis of the novel and film *Psycho*. For the first time such violent anti-heroes were given the limelight. There have been many similar novels and films since, including *10 Rillington Place*, based on Christie; *In Cold Blood*, 1967; *The Boston Strangler*, starring Tony Curtis, in 1968; *The Honeymoon Killers* in 1970; and so on.

The Silence of the Lambs is the best of the films because it is firmly rooted in reality. The device of having the killer lure his victims with his arm in a fake plaster cast was borrowed from the real-life Ted Bundy ploy. The plot is stomach-churning. Trainee FBI agent Clarice Starling (Jodie Foster) has to catch 'Buffalo Bill', a killer of five women who flays his victims so he can wear their skins. She is sent to interview Dr Hannibal Lecter in prison, nicknamed 'Hannibal the Cannibal' because of his penchant for eating his victims. Played with realistic malevolence by Anthony Hopkins, Lecter is a psychiatrist who is also a genius – if a killer. In exchange for the agent feeding him bits of her own life, Lecter supplies clues to the identity of Buffalo Bill. But, of course, there is a twist . . .

The agent tries to understand how a brilliant man like Lecter could have killed nine people and asks what happened to change him. 'Nothing happened to me, Officer Starling. I happened. You can't reduce me to a set of influences . . . A census taker tried to quantify me once. I ate his liver with some beans . . . '

But there is a passage where Lecter attempts to explain himself. 'You created me,' he says. 'All that talk about breaking away from the timid compromises of bourgeois morality, all those grand liberal gestures – all that sex wherever you looked – I am the monstrous result.' And he has a point.

Norman Mailer, in his celebrated essay *The White Negro*, urged us to 'liberate the psychopath within oneself'. The sixties was a period when everyone was advised to 'turn on' to drugs and sex, and morality was rejected as being 'old-fashioned'. There was nothing new in this either. The Marquis de Sade had advocated the same beliefs two hundred years ago in such books as *Philosophy in the Bedroom*, arguing with passionate logic that everyone ought to be able to do his own thing – in his case it was torturing women.

Frederick Nietzsche, the German philosopher of the last century, advised his followers to go *Beyond Good and Evil* (the title of one of his books). Two of his latter-day disciples, Leopold and Loeb, believed in the Nietzschean philosophy of the 'Superman', the man of the future who is above the rules which govern ordinary men and makes his own morality. They were reading Nietzsche at university when they decided to put his philosophy into practice and in 1925 in Chicago they kidnapped and killed little Bobby Franks to demonstrate their 'superiority'. Needless to say, they were quickly caught because they were not supermen but inept criminals. And Nietzsche died insane.

In the film, Hannibal the Cannibal is portrayed as a caged panther with the mind of a computer. When he blames us for creating him, the truth is that he has dared to explore the forbidden zones; he has gone beyond good and evil into a realm where we dare not follow.

Richard Ramirez, the 'Night Stalker', sneered at the court in Los Angeles which recently sentenced him for the murder of twelve people: 'You maggots make me sick. I am beyond your experience.' There is massive vanity here, a contempt for the rest of us. But to learn what he has learned, to go where he has been, you have to become insane.

That statement 'You maggots' is reminiscent of the

journal entries made by Ian Brady. He too had read De Sade avidly and had constructed a warped personal philosophy in which other people were 'morons, cabbages, not deserving to live. People are like maggots, small, blind and worthless.'

Charles Manson made the same challenge to us when he said: 'The children who come at you with knives – they are *your* children – you taught them.' In other words, society is to blame: greedy, uncaring, lax society. This society is captured in *American Psycho*, the gruesome novel by Bret Easton Ellis. The main character is a young Wall Street broker who spends his evenings watching hard-core porn or killing people. His victims are mainly women, but include men, children and even dogs. He casually operates on a girl's face with a power drill, gouges out the eyes from a tramp, leaving bodies in his wake like dandruff. It is his idea of fun. Just as consumer items have become disposable, then in his society people have become disposable too. Since women are victimized in the novel, it has led to women's groups in America ceremonially burning the book in public, and the author has received death threats. But the ultimate question remains unanswered: What do such novels and films tell us about ourselves?

Henry: Portrait of a Serial Killer, director John McNaughton's film based on Henry Lee Lucas – self-confessed killer of 360 people – shows us a few days in the life of a killer in Chicago who kills people to make himself feel better. He introduces his friend Otis to this hobby, and they video-tape themselves torturing and killing their victims, then go home and have a beer in front of the television, watching their video. After the first joint killing, Henry asks Otis: 'Feel better now?' It is no surprise to learn that at the first public screening, fifteen per cent of the audience walked out in disgust.

Of course, the reality of the serial killer – and they currently account for five hundred murders a year in the United States, with thirty to thirty-five serial killers

201

operating at any one time – is that he is so *ordinary*. Christopher Wilder, millionaire killer of eight women, was described by those who knew him as 'just an easy-going quiet guy'. Ted Bundy was a clever law student who happened to kill twenty-three women. Dennis Nilsen, killer of fifteen young men in London, worked at a Job Centre. Peter Sutcliffe, killer of thirteen women, was a lorry-driver. All of them lacked the seductive glamour of the killer on the big screen. The very names given to these demons are so ordinary: Gary, Frank, Henry, Harry, Jack, Peter . . . names of the man next door. As Sutcliffe showed, your neighbour might even be *married* to him.

And that is the problem with films about serial killers. Tony Curtis played the Boston Strangler, Anthony Hopkins the cannibal Dr Lecter, who was based on a composite of Ed Gein and Henry Lee Lucas. But Curtis and Hopkins are real people, people we admire, role models. There is something intrinsically false in having them play real-life killers who are neither role models nor admirable. To exploit human suffering for commercial gain is to trivialize the crimes of the killers.

Perhaps giving publicity to such demons is counterproductive; perhaps they do not deserve to be glamourized; but the fact is, ever since Bram Stoker published *Dracula* a century ago, people have shown an astonishing capacity to love being frightened. We do well to be frightened by the real-life cases, but possibly we can learn from studying them.

What does the case of Heidnik tell us? He exhibited the classic traits of the power fantasist. He even shackled his victims, just as slaves used to be shackled. And why prostitutes and mentally retarded women? Because he had to feel that the women were beneath him, that he was their master.

And now we have our final clue. Why do some killers eat their victims? Because it is the ultimate form of power. To consume the victim is to totally possess them –

forever. It is important to keep in mind the will-to-power motive when reading about Heidnik.

The pornography of an age reflects its fears and fantasies, and modern pornography seems to be a perversion of the will-to-power. It may be argued that it is not too different from the writings of De Sade or Nietzsche – but they were unique in their age, and their sick philosophy is now commonplace.

John Fowles's powerful novel, *The Collector*, is not pornography but literature. However, even literature can inspire devotees to act out the fictional fantasy. The novel is a clinically obsessive study of a man who wins the pools and puts his fantasy into action. He buys a house in an isolated spot, has the basement turned into a prison cell, and then 'collects' a girl and keeps her prisoner in his private dungeon. The pleasure he derives from his captive is compared to that felt by a fanatical butterfly collector with a rare specimen, but what comes across so strongly in the book is the man's sheer power-kick of having a woman completely submissive to his dominant will. The book, which was a best-seller in 1963 and was later filmed, seemed to capture something of the spirit of its age: a feeling that women should exist only to serve the whims of men, and in a sense the novel was a prophecy which was to be fulfilled in America in 1987, in a case which the press called Philadelphia's House of Horror.

At almost midnight on 24 March 1987, a black prostitute, Josefina Rivera, banged hysterically on the door of her boyfriend's apartment in Philadelphia. He had not seen her for four months, since she had gone out on a November evening to turn a trick. He was shocked to see how much she had changed; she looked thin and haggard and had deep scars and sores around her ankles.

The boyfriend, Vincent Nelson, said later: 'She came in, she was rambling on, you know, talking real fast about this guy having three girls chained up in the

203

basement of this house and she was held hostage for four months . . . She said he was beating them, raping them, and had them eating dead people . . . Dog was in the yard eating people bones. I just thought she was crazy . . .'

However, he and the girl went to a phone box and rang the emergency number for the police. Two officers arrived in a squad car and listened to her story. They were initially sceptical, thinking she was perhaps on drugs, but the scars around her ankles convinced them it was a story worth checking out. She said she had been kidnapped on 26 November 1986 by a bearded white man driving a Cadillac Coupé de Ville. He was well-dressed and wearing a Rolex watch. The house in which she said she had been held was just three blocks away. She claimed she had been tortured and sexually abused and had seen other women in the house being treated in a similar fashion. She had also witnessed the murders of two of her fellow-captives . . .

Police kept the house under observation while a warrant was obtained and a search team of officers assembled. The two-storey brick house was in a white working-class neighbourhood and had bars over its windows. On the outside was a placard reading *United Church of the Ministers of God*, and the house was guarded by two fierce dogs, a German shepherd and a Doberman. The address – 3520 North Marshall Street – seems destined to go down in the annals of murder with the same horrific impact as did 10 Rillington Place in British folk-lore.

Police forced entry into the house at 4.30 a.m. on 25 March and were confronted by a bearded white man, who raised his arms when he saw drawn guns. He gave his name as Gary Michael Heidnik, aged forty-three. He was taken into custody and removed to the Sex Crimes Unit at Headquarters. He seemed to think the police had called about his late alimony payments . . .

In the basement the police found two naked black

women. They were chained to a sewer pipe and had shackles on their ankles. They were terrified at first, but when they realized it was the police, they cried out in joy: 'Hosanna – we are free!' and kissed the officers' hands in gratitude.

Sergeant Frank McCloskey asked them: 'Is anyone here but you?' The two women, one aged eighteen, the other twenty-four, pointed to a board on the floor.

'She's there. She's in the hole.'

Pushing the board aside the officer discovered a pit in which crouched yet another naked black woman. She was shackled, but her hands were also cuffed behind her back. She was so weak she had to be lifted out of the hole – and immediately started screaming.

'It's all right,' the other two women assured her. 'It's the police. We're free.'

Still in shock, the woman who had been in the hole began shouting: 'He took my thirty dollars. Get my money back!'

Police had to use bolt-cutters to remove the shackles, and the women were rushed to hospital. All were extremely thin and weak, and covered with bruises. The police now searched the house, finding a stack of pornographic magazines all featuring black women. On the stove was a blackened cooking-pot, its interior covered in a thick crust. One officer opened the fridge and was confronted by a human forearm. That did it. He ran outside and vomited. The officers sent for forensic experts from the Medical Examiner's Office to assist them. One officer at the scene, Detective Lamont Anderson, told reporters that 'other body parts' had been found in the house and it was believed that at least two women had been killed in the basement.

The following day the newspapers all led with lurid headlines which tried to include the elements of murder, rape, bondage, torture and cannibalism. It was known from early on that Heidnik was a 'bishop' in his own invented church and had extensive dealings with the stock exchange – he was worth in excess of half a million dollars and had a Rolls-Royce in the garage of his run-down home. Newspapers called him the 'Rolls-Royce Reverend' and stated that he was into 'stocks and bond-age'. Other headlines declared: MAN HELD IN TORTURE KILLINGS, MADMAN'S SEX ORGY WITH CHAINED WOMEN, and WOMEN CHAINED IN HORROR DUNGEON.

While police continued to take cardboard boxes from the house filled with human remains, and bloodstained clothing and an aluminium cooking-pot among other evidence, the four surviving captives were questioned in hospital and the full sickening details of their ordeal emerged. Three of the women had been imprisoned for three months, tortured and raped daily by the man, who fed them only dog food and bread and water. They were kept as sex-slaves in the basement, being released from their shackles only when they were taken upstairs for further sex and torture. Police were revolted to learn that at times the starving captives had been fed on human flesh put through a food-processor and blended with the dog food. A dog had been seen chewing on a human leg . . .

One of the women led police to where another woman's body lay buried. One of the survivors, nineteen-year-old Lisa Thomas, told of having seen a woman she knew only as 'Sandy' fall while handcuffed to a chain from the ceiling and strike her head a fatal blow on the concrete floor. Sandy was later identified as Sandra Lindsay, aged twenty-four. Miss Rivera, the woman who had raised the alarm, told police that the man had boas-ted of having fed the boiled remains of Sandy to the starving women. Police were also told of how twenty-three-year-old Debbie Johnson had been murdered. She had been placed in a pit filled with water and electrocuted by wires attached to her chains. That pit served another purpose; it was the 'hole' in which the captives were kept when being punished, and to prevent escape. Whenever 'the master' left the house a wooden board was placed over it, held down by a sack of sand.

The story which emerged sounded like the plot of De Sade's *Justine*, written two hundred years ago. The man lured the women to his house one at a time to hold them as sex-slaves. He drove expensive cars and had plenty of money to flash around. In fact, the walls of his bedroom were papered with one- and five-dollar bills.

Josefina Rivera was the first captive, picked up on 26 November 1986 for sex. Heidnik drove her to his house and, after sex, began to throttle her into submission. He handcuffed her and took her down to the basement and shackled her by the ankle. She watched as he dug a large hole in the concrete floor, fearing it was to be her grave. He reassured her: the hole was only for punishment if she misbehaved. He confided that he was only attracted to black women, and his ambition was to have ten women captive in the cellar and have children by them all. 'We'll all be one big happy family,' he promised.

He also told her that he had served four years in prison after being found guilty of the rape of a mentally retarded black woman by whom he wanted to have a child. It was unfair, he said, because the sex had been voluntary, and the daughter he had by the woman had been placed in a home. 'Society owes me a wife and family,' he told his captive. He then forced her to perform oral sex on him, before having vaginal sex.

Later that day Josefina managed to force open a boarded-over window and screamed for help. Nobody paid her any attention. Heidnik heard her and came down and beat her, before throwing her into the hole. He left her with a radio playing rock music at full volume to drown any cries for help.

On 29 November – three days later – Heidnik brought his second captive down into the basement. Sandra Lindsay had known Heidnik for years and had once been pregnant by him. He had been furious when he learned she had had an abortion. Heidnik forced her to write to her mother, saying she was all right, and later posted the letter from New York.

The basement was cold, lit only by a naked bulb, with the floor covered in litter. The routine each day was the same: beatings and forced sex, a prison diet of oatmeal and bread. Later Heidnik began feeding the women dog food from tins, which he spread on bread. One by one the other captives were brought down to the basement. On 22 December Lisa Thomas was captured. She said she had been accosted by a white man sitting in a Lincoln and had accepted his invitation to dinner. Afterwards she agreed to go to his home to watch some video-tapes. 'Then I fell asleep and the next thing I know he was choking me and he handcuffed me. He took me down to the basement and put chains on my legs. He beat me with a wooden stick. There were two other women down there. They were chained too.'

Later, two more girls were brought down to the basement to be chained. On 1 January 1987 Deborah Dudley joined the other three. Heidnik came to regret this. Debbie was a stronger character and argued back, inciting the other girls to revolt. Heidnik had to beat her frequently. On 18 January eighteen-year-old Jacquelyn Askins was captured. Her ankles were so thin that she could not be shackled, and Heidnik had to use handcuffs.

By now Heidnik was treating Josefina Rivera as a 'trusty'. She was allowed out of the cellar to have meals with him, and kept discipline among the other captives. She reported any talk of escape attempts. On 23 March Heidnik took her out in his car with him, and together they picked up yet another captive, Agnes Adams, aged twenty-four, another prostitute. She was needed because by then two of the other captives were dead.

On 7 February Sandra Lindsay had died. She had been suspended by her hands from the ceiling for a week as a punishment for attempting to escape from the hole. She had died from sheer exhaustion. On 18 March Heidnik filled the hole with water and made the women – with the exception of Josefina – climb in, then tortured them with electric shocks from a bare wire. It touched Deborah Dudley's chains and she was killed instantly.

Heidnik had disposed of Sandra by putting her body through a meat-grinder and boiling her head in a pan on the stove. Neighbours complained of the stench of cooking meat, but Heidnik told an investigating policeman that he had burnt his dinner. The officer did not bother to look in the saucepan on the stove.

Next came another refinement in cruelty. To make the girls deaf so that they would not hear any rescue attempt, Heidnik jabbed a screwdriver into their ears, twisting it around to rupture the ear drums. Josefina was not subjected to this. She had by now gained Heidnik's trust by snitching on the other girls and beating them on Heidnik's orders. He often took her out to fast-food restaurants for meals or for a ride in his Cadillac or Rolls-Royce. She had been with him when he buried Deborah Dudley in a New Jersey park on 22 March. On the way back Heidnik had stopped to buy a newspaper. 'I want to check my stocks,' he told his unwilling accomplice. Hardly the action of a madman, to check the stock-market prices after disposing of a murder victim.

By then Rivera had become so trusted that she persuaded Heidnik that it was time she went to see her family to put their minds at rest. She promised to return . . . On 24 March Heidnik dropped her off at the very corner where he had picked her up four months previously, and she immediately rushed to her boyfriend's apartment and babbled out her weird tale.

When arrested, Heidnik was found to have almost two thousand dollars on him, and numerous credit cards. There were papers for four cars, and a statement from the stockbrokers Merill Lynch showing his account standing at $577,382.52. On 25 March, within hours of his arrest, Heidnik was attacked by revolted fellow-prisoners and had his nose broken. Placed in isolation for his own protection, on 2 April he attempted to hang himself in the shower but was rescued unconscious.

Police continued to search the murder house, dredging the sewers and tearing apart the walls in search of further bodies. They had already recovered parts of the dismembered body of a girl wrapped in plastic from the freezer, but they were seeking a third body. Meanwhile, other detectives began investigating Heidnik's background. The wealthy self-styled 'bishop' insisted that police call him 'Reverend'. He had a record for violence, having been charged the previous year with 'spouse rape' by his wife, who had since left him. Police estabished that Heidnik's *modus operandi* was to seduce women with a mixture of religion and kindness – and then terrorize them with sadism.

Born in November 1943 in Cleveland, Heidnik was the archetypal serial killer. He was the product of a broken home; his parents separated when he was two years old and his mother committed suicide in 1970 when she learned she had cancer. He had not seen his father in twenty years. As a child he had been an object of ridicule because of the shape of his head: classmates called him 'football head', but the shape had been caused by injuries following a fall from a tree. (A high proportion of serial killers have a history of head injuries.) Heidnik had a loveless childhood, which he spent in a fantasy world of his own. He was also a bed-wetter, a fact which enraged his heavy-drinking father, who beat him often. Following the arrest of his son, the father told the press: 'I hope to hell they hang him, and you can quote me on that. I'll even pull the rope.'

Gary Heidnik's younger brother, forty-one-year-old Terry, gave an interesting insight into the Jekyll-and-Hyde character who had been labelled the 'Beast of Philadelphia'. Terry Heidnik said that he and his brother had been raised in a family atmosphere of violence and racism. It was an unhappy childhood. They were taught by their father that 'life has no value if it's a black life'. The father's prejudice stemmed from the affairs his alcoholic wife had with black men after the couple divorced in 1946. Gary Heidnik had adopted the racial attitudes of his father. All his victims were black, and the very act of shackling them was to treat them as slaves had been treated.

Heidnik was a high-school drop-out who enrolled in the Army for three years. Here he became a loan-shark and made money. His childhood fantasies had always centred around money, on dreams of becoming a millionaire. On 25 August 1962 he complained to an Army doctor of headaches and dizzy spells. He was diagnosed as being either schizoid or schizophrenic. On 23 January 1963 he was given an honourable discharge and awarded a one hundred per cent mental disability pension for life, his condition being considered service-related. He had served just fourteen months of his enlistment. For over twenty years Heidnik lived on this, some two thousand dollars a month plus social security payments.

Following his discharge Heidnik settled in Philadelphia. At first he tried to gain credits at the University of Pennsylvania in a number of subjects, his IQ being 130, or thirty above average. His attempts to live first with his mother, then his father, were failures. His father did not want him in his life. He drifted from job to job, finally becoming a male nurse. He never lasted long. In the years which followed he was admitted to mental hospitals at least twenty-one times and attempted suicide on thirteen occasions. In the spring of 1971 he founded his own church, registering it as a charity with himself as bishop for life. He seems to have held genuine services with his flock, but his church's money-raising ventures included bingo and loan-sharking. In 1975 he opened an account with Merrill Lynch in the name of his church, and began playing the stock market with remarkable success. By 1976 he was a wealthy man. In that same year came his first arrest for carrying a firearm on a public street. He had rented an apartment to a man, but

211

when the man climbed in the window one night, Heidnik fired at him with a revolver. The charge of assault with a deadly weapon was dropped.

By March 1978 Heidnik had become a father; a mentally retarded black woman had borne his child. Her sister was in a mental institution and on 7 May 1978 Heidnik broke her out and hid her at his home. He considered he was doing her a favour. When the police came looking for her, they found her hidden in Heidnik's basement. There was a quantity of pornographic material in the house, and it was obvious that the girl had been sexually abused. Since she had a venereal infection of the throat, oral sex was not hard to prove and Heidnik was convicted of unlawful imprisonment and deviate sex. In November 1978 he was sentenced to three to seven years in the state penitentiary, of which he served four years. He was released on parole on 12 April 1983, aged forty.

He bought the house at 3520 North Marshall Street and became noted for his extraordinary sexual behaviour. Every night he seemed to have three-in-a-bed sex, sometimes with women from his congregation. It was always black women with him and always deviate sex. Deciding he wanted a Filipino wife, he went to a matrimonial agency, and Betty Disto flew from Manila to Philadelphia to join him. They were married within three days. A week later she came home from shopping to find him in bed with three women. Heidnik tried to assure her that this was a normal custom for American males, but after being subjected to forced sodomy she left him in January 1986. A court ordered him to pay her 135 dollars a week. In November of that same year Heidnik began stocking his harem, first kidnapping Josefina Rivera . . .

The trial of Gary Heidnik began on 20 June 1988 in Philadelphia City Hall, room 653, before a woman judge, Lynn M. Abraham. It was obvious from the start that the defence tactic would be to claim insanity, but the prosecutor, Assistant District Attorney Charles Gallagher made it plain long before the trial that he would seek the death penalty. The defence counsel was Charles Peruto, a flamboyant lawyer with a good record of acquittals; but in this case he was fighting a losing battle.

It had taken a long time to choose a jury, the defence were seeking an all-white jury for some reason. The prosecutor made his opening statement, telling the jury that Heidnik had murdered, raped, kidnapped and assaulted six young women between the ages of eighteen and twenty-five. 'Gary Heidnik took these women home with him,' Gallagher said. 'He plied them with food and in some cases sex. He assaulted them. He choked them. He handcuffed them and took them to his basement, where he put shackles on their ankles . . . He starved them. He tortured them. He repeatedly had sex with them.' He added that Heidnik had killed two of them, one of whose bodies he dismembered, cooked, and fed to the others. The jury looked green. 'The evidence will show that from the eve of Thanksgiving 1986 up through 25 March 1987, the defendant committed repeated and sadistic malicious acts. He did them in a methodical and systematic way. He knew exactly what he was doing and he knew it was wrong. He took advantage of underprivileged people.'

When the defence counsel rose, the judge reminded him that he need not make an opening statement; that his client was innocent until proved guilty. Peruto retorted: 'My client is not innocent. He is very, very guilty.' He said his client had indeed done all the things he had been accused of, but said that while the prosecutor had promised to construct a trail of evidence leading right to Heidnik's door, he didn't want to stop there. He wanted to take the jury through that door and show the man inside.

'There's no mystery here,' he went on. 'This is not a whodunit. If all we had to decide here was who did it and what was done, it would be easy. You're not here to determine if Gary Heidnik is going to walk out of here a free man. He's never going to see the light of day. He will be put behind bars or in some mental institution. Any person who puts dog food and human remains in a food processor and calls it a gourmet meal and feeds it to others is out to lunch.'

Peruto said the defence would be one of insanity, telling the jury that he would be calling expert witnesses to testify to that fact. 'Understand two things,' he told the jury. 'One, Gary Heidnik didn't want anybody to die, and two, because of his mental illness he couldn't tell right from wrong.'

The witnesses were called, one by one. Josefina Rivera was asked what the women had done to pass the time in the basement.

'Nothing too much . . . outside of just having sex and staying in the hole. Three times we were down in the hole and we ran out of air and couldn't breathe. We started screaming and hollering and Gary came down and beat us . . . We didn't take any baths or wash our hair . . . Music was going twenty-four hours a day.'

Telling of the death of Sandra Lindsay, she said: 'He carried her body upstairs and we heard an electric saw, then we smelled a terrible odour. He smelled like it and so did the food he brought us.' She said that Heidnik stopped beating her in January because he was beginning to feel he could trust her. But he was having problems with Debbie Dudley. 'He always had trouble with Debbie . . . Debbie always fought back.' Not long after Lindsay died, Heidnik took Debbie upstairs. 'In about five minutes she came back. She was very quiet.' Rivera said she asked her what had happened, and Dudley told her: 'He showed me Sandra's head cooking in a pot, and her ribs were cooking in a roasting pan in the stove, and her legs and arms were in the freezer. He told me if I didn't start listening to him, that would happen to me . . .' Six weeks later she too was dead.

Rivera continued her testimony. 'Everybody went on punishment in early March. We were eating dog food mixed with body parts.' She was asked if she knew where Heidnik got his ideas from, and replied brightly: 'Yes. He got them from watching movies and TV. He got the idea of feeding us parts of Sandy's body from *Eating Raoul*, and his ideas on punishment from *Mutiny on the Bounty*. He also saw *The World of Susie Wong* and he liked the way Oriental women were. That's why he picked a Filipino wife.'

Lisa Thomas was the next witness. The day after he first shackled her, Heidnik seemed to have a touch of compassion and fitted a longer chain between her ankles. 'Why did he do that?' Gallagher asked.

'So I could open my legs wider to have sex,' she replied.

'Did he beat you too?'

'Yes, almost from the first moment. He hit me five times with a thick brown stick . . . He told me to beat Sandy regularly; he'd get his kicks from seeing us beat each other . . . '

Jacquelyn Askins was the youngest of the witnesses, still only nineteen when she took the stand. She looked frightened to death as she described the sex-parties Heidnik forced her to join in from her basement cell. She also told of the frequent beating she endured, and of having to eat dog food sandwiches.

The remaining witnesses were policemen and doctors. Detectives told of what they found in Heidnik's house; Dr Robert Catherman, who performed the autopsy on Dudley, confirmed that she had died of electrocution. 'It was an almost classic example of electrothermal injury,' he said. The irony of this was that if found guilty, Heidnik would die in exactly the same way as his victim.

Dr Paul Hoyer had examined the body part removed from Heidnik's freezer. He testified that he had found in the yard a bone covered in dog hairs. It was from an upper left arm and matched the other body parts found in the freezer, which included several ribs, a number of tooth fragments and one whole tooth. Positive identification of the remains came from a wrist found in the

215

freezer. Lindsay had injured her wrist a year earlier and her X-ray was on file. 'The overall size and shape matched, plus the pattern matched. There is a pattern in bone and each pattern is unique. By comparing this we were able to say this was Sandra Lindsay.' The prosecution rested its case.

One psychiatrist called by the defence, Dr Clancy McKenzie, argued that there existed within Heidnik's head an adult brain and a brain only seventeen months old. It was the infantile part of the brain which had kidnapped and raped women. Heidnik was a schizophrenic, he declared firmly. The judge was openly sceptical of this explanation. The judge ruled that the defence could not call in evidence of Heidnik's twenty-year history of mental illness, nor even produce the records from various doctors in evidence. It was a blow which sank the defence.

A broker from Merrill Lynch said that 'Bishop' Heidnik opened an account with a cheque for fifteen hundred dollars. Over the next seven years Heidnik bought shares over the telephone, and his original stake increased to over half a million dollars. The prosecutor asked the witness: 'What kind of investor was he?'

'A very astute investor,' was the reply.

The defence made its closing speech. Peruto told the jury: 'What was Gary Heidnik's purpose? His purpose was to raise ten kids, not to kill anybody. Third-degree murder is reckless disregard for human life. This is a classic case of third degree.'

He said that of his captives, one was retarded and three were prostitutes. 'As sick as it is, these were his chosen people. These were the girls he wanted to reproduce with. Is that sane? It's a case of Dr Jekyll and Mr Heidnik. Isn't it more likely that he's insane than not? . . . What kind of mentality does it take to have human flesh in front of you. A human being. And to cut through that body. To cut through flesh. To cut through bone and to take some of those body parts and wrap them up and put them in the freezer. And then to cook some and feed it to the others. Who was he trying to impress with that delusion?' He demanded a verdict of not guilty by reason of insanity.

The prosecutor made his reply. Gallagher said that Heidnik planned each of the abductions, he killed in a cold, premeditated fashion and disposed of Lindsay's body by dismembering it and cooking the parts which could lead to her identification – the head and the hands. 'Just because someone does bizarre acts, the law doesn't recognize them as insane . . . What he did was premeditated, deliberate murder.'

On 1 July 1988 the jury found Heidnik guilty in the first degree on all counts in the indictment. They then went away to consider the penalty phase. Under Pennsylvanian law, the jury that returns a Guilty verdict for first-degree murder must also decide the penalty. They have two choices: life in prison, or death in the electric chair. The jury returned the following day with a decision of death.

Peruto was angry, insisting that the jury had acted emotionally, not intellectually. He asked the judge to issue an order to prison officials to make sure Heidnik was kept in isolation. 'If he is put in the general population, the jury's wishes will be carried out immediately,' he warned.

Judge Abraham said: 'If your client is going to commit suicide, he's going to do it. Prison officials don't want that, but neither do they want prisoners killing other prisoners. I don't have the authority to order him held in isolation, but I will suggest they carefully watch him for suicide and carefully house him.'

She then immediately sentenced Heidnik to death for the murder of Lindsay, setting a date three months ahead for sentencing on the Dudley killing. A reporter telephoned Heidnik's father with the news and asked for his reaction. The father replied: 'I'm not interested. I don't care. It don't bother me a bit.'

Heidnik fits the pattern of the serial killer exactly, with his early history of disturbed childhood and bed-wetting. And because he felt sexually incompetent, chose women: in order to feel potent he had to have women whom he felt were 'below' him, nothing more than sex-slaves.

He suffered from low self-esteem. To counter this, he founded his own church. He gave himself a role in life, and invented his own rules. But when his wife left him, the rejection shattered his self-image. He would make sure a woman would never leave him again – he would *chain* them.

To found your own church is to make your own rules. There, in that mad church, the bishop and the murderer could coexist, he was ordained by God, all his actions justified by divine command. He could rape and kill and torture with total moral self-approval.

Gary Heidnik sits on death row in the State Correctional Institution at Pittsburgh, now simply prisoner number F1398. He eats alone, showers alone, and is watched at all times lest he cheat the executioner. He was attacked by other prisoners on the way to prison and severely beaten. Still, it was nothing compared to what he did to his victims.

Heidnik is an authentic human monster, but sheer horror at his actions should not excuse us from looking for the truth. And the truth must be that he was as mad as a hatter for years. Twenty-one times in mental institutions, twenty-one times released. He never should have been released . . . Psychiatry is not an exact science and experts will disagree, but it is plain that Heidnik was mad. And no civilized nation executes madmen.

Heidnik will have years to wait for his execution – if it ever comes. In the meantime he is as caged as he caged his victims; and while he is in the cage we should study him, learn from him, try to enter the icy madness of his mind and see if we see ourselves reflected there. Dr Lecter in *The Silence of the Lambs* was a fictional character. Heidnik is all too real: our very own living nightmare.

How many other like him are there out there? There's
the rub . . .

10
MODERN AMERICAN CANNIBALS

Recent cannibal murders in the United States include one which has strong echoes of the Ed Gein case. It took place in the same central plains of Wisconsin, in a small town called Phillips.

Carla Lenz, a pretty seventeen-year-old pupil at Phillips High School, vanished on 12 November 1986, just before she was due to graduate. It seemed unlikely that she had run away from home, since a search of her room revealed that she had left behind all her clothes and toiletries, together with a wallet containing her identification and a cheque book and cash. The search for the missing girl was protracted, but it came to nothing.

Then, on 4 September 1988 – twenty-two months later – Carla's brother-in-law John Weber telephoned the police to report that his wife had been abducted by two men in a car, and had been raped and savagely beaten. She had arrived home in the early hours, looking like something from a horror movie. Her head was swollen up like a football from multiple blows, her eyes were closed and blackened, and she had knife wounds to her body.

Police Chief Moore wondered why Weber had waited a full day before reporting the attack on his wife; he claimed he had been busy tending her wounds. The officer questioned the wife in her hospital bed without the presence of the husband, and whatever script her husband had concocted for her, she departed from it and told the truth.

220

Her husband had driven her to a dirt road on the pretext of showing her a house they might want to buy. He had stopped the car and ordered her to write a letter to her mother and sign several cheques, before tying her up and raping her. He had then dragged her body into nearby woods and smashed her in the face twenty or thirty times with the blade of a shovel, before he finally stopped and untied her bonds, begging her forgiveness. He didn't know what had come over him, he claimed. But when he had been beating his wife with that shovel, he had threatened to 'make her disappear like Carla disappeared'.

Detectives were intrigued. When Carla disappeared, Weber had been questioned, as had all her relatives, but he had never been a suspect. Now he had to be viewed in a new light. The following day detectives impounded his car and searched it for any forensic evidence that Carla might have met her death in the vehicle.

What they found was a large hunting knife, a cut-up brassiere and panties from the attack on his wife, and the cheques and letter which Mrs Weber had been forced to write. But the prize find was a tape-recorder in the glove compartment. Detectives switched on the tape and listened. What they heard stunned them.

Speaking in a dull monotone, John Weber began talking about his marital problems with his wife, and admitted his sister-in-law appealed to him. He then described how, on the night of 12 November 1986, he drove her to a remote spot, stuck a gun in her face and ordered her to strip. Then he raped her.

He described fondling her breasts, squeezing them cruelly, and pulling out tufts of her pubic hair, before burning her nipples with a lighted cigarette. 'I wanted to stop, but I couldn't,' Weber said brokenly. 'I wanted to go home, but the evil part of me wouldn't let me.'

He pulled the girl from his car into woodland and raped her, anally and vaginally, simultaneously with two wheelbarrow handles. He then removed these and

221

replaced them with two beer bottles, which he kicked viciously into her body until they disappeared. He held one of her breasts up tautly by the nipple and then sliced the complete breast off, holding it up before Carla's terrified eyes, before choking her to death.

For the next five days he drove around with the body in the boot of his car, wondering how to get rid of it. His taped voice went on: 'I had this wild idea. Her left leg was undamaged, so I took out a knife and cut off her calf, just the muscle. I brought it to the house, washed it, skinned it, and that night I made myself some patties from Carla's leg.'

The breast he had kept in a plastic bag, and he sliced this up and cooked it. 'I figured I'd like to try a woman's breast,' his voice continued, 'so I did. And you know, human meat doesn't taste that bad. I was surprised. Actually it tasted good.'

Faced with the evidence of his own confession on the tape, Weber showed the police where he had eventually buried Carla, and her remains were recovered. Weber was charged with the murder of his sister-in-law and the assault and rape of his wife.

At his court hearing, his defence lawyers managed to get a change of venue and persuaded the judge to issue an order restraining the prosecution from mentioning cannibalism or making any reference to Ed Gein. The prosecution agreed to abide by this ruling.

The trial of Weber took place in March 1989, when he pleaded guilty to killing Carla Lenz and attempting to kill his wife. However, there were nine further charges to answer, and the jury got to hear that tape.

When it was played in the hushed courtroom, the jury were obviously stunned. They took just over two hours to find Weber guilty on nine counts of false imprisonment, sexual dismemberment, and seven counts of sexual assault in connection with the attack on his sister-in-law.

The penalty phase of the trial took place on 14 March, with the defence counsel pleading that Weber was a very sick man who suffered from a mental illness: he was a sexual sadist. 'John Weber, since a very young age, has built up an elaborate mechanism to deal with that illness. John has covered, concealed, lied and distorted to keep his secret hidden. This camouflage continues to this day as he tries to maintain an outward appearance of being normal.'

Evidence was heard that from the age of five Weber had shown an interest in dressing in his grandmother's clothing, and had progressed from that to an avid interest in pornography and sexual violence. A relative told of finding bondage magazines in his room when he was just ten years of age. Psychiatrists testified to Weber's bizarre fantasies and his interst in witchcraft and Satanism.

But on 18 March 1989, the jury returned a verdict that Weber had been sane when he tortured and murdered his sister-in-law and attempted to murder his wife. He was sentenced to life imprisonment with no possibility of parole.

The second case comes from New York City, the seedy area around the Port Authority bus terminal known as 'Alphabet City', haunt of twangy boys and baby prostitutes, chicken hawks and queer bashers, and hustlers and grifters of every description.

Around this area – along Ninth Street in the East Village and nearby Tompkins Square Park – officers of the Ninth and Tenth precincts began to hear rumours of a particularly nasty homicide. The essence of the story, often repeated by drug addicts whose brains were scrambled anyway, was that a young girl who worked as an exotic dancer had disappeared from her room on East Ninth Street in August 1989. No one had seen her alive since, but a former roommate had visited her and found her decapitated torso in the bath, and when she lifted the lid off a pot on the cooker, she discovered her friend's severed head, the sightless eyes staring at her.

That was it: a crazy story told by junkies. Police

officers listened, but they were not impressed or horrified. New York was a very weird place anyway, and this was just a rumour.

But one cop did listen. Detective Richard Abbinanti was on duty in Tompkins Square Park on Friday, 8 September 1989, investigating another case, when a young woman approached him and told him the story of the missing dancer. The woman began by asking him if he had heard about the murder on Ninth Street on 19 August. The detective hadn't, and he encouraged the girl to continue. She told him a sickening story full of detail about the murder – and hinted at the identity of the killer.

That was enough. Abbinanti, together with his partner, Detective James Theis, searched the apartment of the missing girl. Monica Beerle was a twenty-six-year-old Swiss national who had come to the United States to further her career and had been attending classes at the Martha Graham Centre for Contemporary Dance. She had lived at the Ninth Street address for about two months.

Checking revealed that she had not attended classes since 19 August. Relatives in Switzerland were contacted, but no one had heard anything from the missing woman. Now the search for her began in earnest. The apartment revealed no clues to the woman's fate. The bath was dismantled and examined, but there was no blood in the U-bend.

Eventually the friend who had seen Monica's head in a cooking pot on the stove was found. It had been no crack-smoker's dream; she really had seen the head, but said she had been too terrified to report her grisly find to the police. Monica's big blond boyfriend was scary.

Witnesses were found who had seen Monica's boyfriend on the day she disappeared. He was Daniel Rakowitz, a bearded Texan of twenty-eight who went around with dead chickens hanging from his neck. He was not exactly a figure to be forgotten. He had been seen dragging the missing woman's belongings from her apartment and dumping them on the street for the garbage collection.

When approached by a friend and asked what he was doing, Rakowitz had mumbled: 'The bitch attacked me, she scratched me, then I hit her and killed her. I didn't mean it, but I killed her. It got out of hand. I killed her and boiled her head. Then I made soup out of her brains. It tasted pretty good.'

Deputy Police Chief Ronald Fenrich, head of Manhattan detectives, had now taken over supervision of the case, and his first priority was to find Rakowitz.

The suspect was located on Monday, 18 September, in a Brooklyn restaurant. He was arrested and taken to Manhattan. After questioning at police headquarters, Rakowitz produced a claim ticket for the left luggage counter in the bus terminal and said: 'I have a bag there. If you open it and look inside, you'll see her bones.' He spoke calmly, as if commenting on the weather.

The bag was claimed by detectives, a large green duffel bag which was holding a five-gallon plastic bucket full of human bones and a skull, human remains which were later to be positively identified as being those of the missing exotic dancer.

On Tuesday, 19 September, Rakowitz was taken before Judge Mary Davis, who was told of his full confession to the brutal murder with which he stood charged. A police source said that it had taken Rakowitz a week to dismember his victim's body, pulling out her teeth with pliers and using an electric kitchen knife, a hacksaw and a wooden chopping block.

Rakowitz was a devil-worshipper who took drugs and claimed to have been on an acid trip when he murdered Monica Beerle. Across the front door to his flat – which he referred to as his 'temple' – he had scrawled messages in paint. *Is it soup yet? Welcome to Charlie Gein's Ranch East*. Another read: *The 700 club. E Ninth St. – Home of the Fine Young Cannibals*. The reference to Ed Gein did not go unnoticed.

The blond, bearded killer was a petty crook who dealt in drugs and had had several relationships with women which depended on a sadistic bonding. With Monica Beerle he simply went too far. He beat her severely, killing her with a karate blow to the throat. Then he plunged a knife twenty times into her slender body, before dismembering her. Now, faced with judgment for his actions, he pleaded insanity and was remanded for psychiatric tests.

These two cases are taken almost at random from detective files, demonstrating that the tradition of cannibalism lives on in the richest nation in the world. Similar examples could be recounted *ad nauseam*.

11

JEFFREY DAHMER: THE MILWAUKEE CANNIBAL

Just when we had got over the stunning success of the film *The Silence of the Lambs*, along came a case which seemed to be a prime example of life imitating art: the 'Milwaukee Cannibal', Jeffrey Dahmer . . .

The Dahmer story began when Tracy Edwards ran out of an apartment building, handcuffs dangling from his wrists, and flagged down a passing police patrol car. Edwards, a black man, aged thirty-two told the police officers how he had been lured to the home of Jeffrey Dahmer, at 213 Oxford Apartments in the predominantly black area of Milwaukee. Dahmer was a white man of thirty-one who worked at a chocolate factory.

It was on the evening of 22 July 1991 that Dahmer met Edwards, a father of six, in a shopping mall and invited him back to his apartment for a beer. Edwards wrinkled his nose at the terrible smell permeating the apartment – which Dahmer explained was due to faulty plumbing – but stayed seven hours. 'He seemed like a regular guy,' Edwards said later.

Edwards would not reveal what they talked about or what happened, except to say that at one point he willingly snapped the handcuffs on to one wrist, but then got scared when he noticed Dahmer's knife.

The police raided Dahmer's apartment as a result of what Edwards told them, and found a chilling scene inside. Swarms of flies hovered over the remains of at least eleven corpses. A soup pan on the stove contained human brains which had been simmered in tomato sauce. In the refrigerator were three human heads wrapped in cling-film, and hands and feet in another pan had apparently been boiled. A number of glass jars in the kitchen contained the genitalia of at least three men, all preserved in a saline solution.

Officers had to wear rubber protective suits and special breathing apparatus to remove the evidence from the flat. Even so, all the officers who entered that chamber of horrors had to undergo specialist counselling to help them recover from the shock.

Officers noticed that there was very little actual food in the apartment, just one or two packets of savoury snacks. It is claimed that Dahmer lived on the flesh of his victims. Newspapers reported that following his arrest, Dahmer confessed to eating the flesh of his victims, describing how he had sliced off a victim's bicep, fried it in vegetable oil, and eaten it.

Over the years Dahmer had killed at least eleven young men in his apartment, it was alleged, dismembering their bodies with the aid of a chainsaw. Police found scores of Polaroid photographs of the nude victims, Dahmer's little souvenirs of his exploits. The photographs were found stuffed down beside bags of dismembered limbs.

Dahmer was a homosexual with a hatred for blacks – he claimed he had been gang-raped by blacks while in prison on a child-molestation charge – and he was that rare serial killer: a man who crossed the racial line to kill. Usually, whites kill whites, and blacks kill blacks. Dahmer had been jailed for eight years in 1989 for child-molesting, but had only served ten months of that sentence before being released in March 1990.

The police came in for criticism when it was revealed that one of Dahmer's victims had earlier tried to escape from his clutches, on 27 May. He had run out of the building, naked and screaming, bleeding from the rectum and begging police officers to rescue him. They had laughed the incident off as a 'homosexual lovers' tiff' and had returned the victim to Dahmer. The victim was a boy aged fourteen years . . .

Police transcripts of the radio call made by the patrol car revealed that the officers involved joked with their dispatcher about the plight of the boy, Konerak Sinthasomphone, reporting: 'Intoxicated Asian, naked male. Was returned to sober boy-friend.' The boy's parents had reported him missing several hours previously.

The adult Dahmer was able to fool the police and his neighbours, but as a child he had not fooled his classmates. They knew him to be a highly disturbed loner. One said: 'By junior high school, everyone gave him a wide berth. He always tried to be the class clown, but his sense of humour was cruel and really dark.

'He would run through shopping malls, acting like he was mentally retarded, just to get people's attention. He didn't win a lot of friends that way.'

After dropping out of high school, Dahmer joined the Army and served a two-year stint in Germany at the US Air Force base at Baumholder, twenty-five miles south-west of Mainz. During this period – between 1979 and 1981 – the remains of five mutilated murder victims were found close to the base. The murders had baffled the German police. Now they are anxious to question Dahmer . . .

Following his release from prison on parole, Dahmer was given a job at the Ambrosia chocolate factory in Milwaukee. He spent his spare time cruising the local seedy gay bars, and was eventually sacked for absenteeism in the summer of 1991. *The Silence of the Lambs* was showing at a local cinema, and Dahmer went to see it.

Reports indicate that Dahmer began killing and eating his victims long before the film was ever made or the novel written. It appears that he committed his first murder shortly after he left school, when he picked up a hitch-hiker, nineteen-year-old Steve Hicks, and battered him with a bar-bell, then strangled him to finish him off.

Dahmer has provided police with a map of the burial site, and human bones have been recovered at the time of writing. But the film did seem to whet his appetite, since most of his victims were butchered, cooked and eaten during the last six weeks prior to his arrest.

When arrested, police found Dahmer polite and co-operative. He told how he lured his victims back to his apartment with promises of sex or free beer. Once he got them inside, he found some way of drugging them, before killing them. Some fought back with phenomenal strength, but Dahmer always prevailed.

Meanwhile, the FBI Behavioural Science Unit in Virginia are the least surprised at the horrifying revelations surrounding this case. Jeffrey Dahmer, they say, fits the serial-killer profile perfectly. According to their psychologists, a serial killer is likely to be a loner, possibly the victim of school bullies, and someone who consistently under-achieves his outward promise. Generally they have been pressurized into setting their goals too high, and resort to lying – even to themselves – to cover their inadequacies and inabilities.

The typical serial killer is white, unlikely to be able to hold down a job for long, with abnormal sexual needs. Such a man would feel a compulsion to treasure trophies of his killings – exactly as Dahmer did. The most chilling aspect in serial killers is their apparent normality. Jeffrey Dahmer, described by his neighbours as a pleasant, polite man, is a reasonably good-looking thirty-one-year-old – clean-cut but unremarkable. He comes from a respectable middle-class family who concerned themselves with his education. As one neighbour said when he discovered what the police had learned about Dahmer: 'Who the hell would have thought we were living with that monster in our building? He's so damn ordinary!'

Prosecutor Michael McCann told reporters about the scene inside Dahmer's apartment, and about his killing of Oliver Lacy, aged twenty-three. 'He dismembered him and placed the man's head in the bottom of the refrigerator – and kept the man's heart in the freezer to eat later.' He claimed that Dahmer was responsible 'for at least seventeen killings'. Through his lawyer, Dahmer issued a terse statement. It read: 'Tell the world I am sorry for what I have done.'

The trial of Dahmer began on 27 January 1992 as the State of Wisconsin vs. Jeffrey Dahmer, Case No. 912542. After the charges had been read out, Dahmer's lawyer, Gerald Boyle, the court-appointed defence counsel, told Judge Gram that although Dahmer admitted killing fifteen young men and boys, he had been insane at the time. Had the court accepted this insanity plea, Dahmer would have been committed to a mental institution for the criminally insane, and after twelve months could have petitioned the courts for his freedom.

'The decision to plead guilty is Dahmer's defence,' Boyle said. 'This case is all about his mental condition.'

The burden of proving that Dahmer was insane fell on the defence, who began calling witnesses to testify to his madness. As a child Dahmer had killed and mutilated a dog, nailing its carcass to a tree. Cruelty to animals in childhood is a key element in the profile of a serial killer. In the course of the three-week hearing, the court heard how Dahmer had cooked and eaten a human heart, a bicep and a thigh. He had cut his victims into handy fist-sized pieces to fit his fridge, after sodomizing some of them.

A doctor testified that Dahmer had attempted to perform crude lobotomies on some of his drugged victims, drilling holes into their skulls and then pouring in acid in the hope of deadening a portion of their brains. 'Dahmer had hoped to control and keep them around longer by turning them into zombie-like creatures,' the doctor said.

Dahmer's counsel told the jury that his client was a 'steam-rolling killing machine' who had been out of control at the time of the killings. There were six expert witnesses to be heard in the case; two for the defence, two for the prosecution, and two appointed by the court. All had interviewed Dahmer. Their testimony in court took a total of some seventeen hours.

The defence presented its case first, with the prosecution to rebut later. Dr Frederick Berlin, a psychiatrist specializing in sexual disorders, said that Dahmer's obsession with having sex with corpses – (necrophilia) – took over his mind and drove him out of control. The doctor said that in his opinion Dahmer did not have the capacity to control or adapt his behaviour to the requirements of the law. 'He lacked the capacity to appreciate the wrongfulness of his actions.'

Defence counsel asked him: 'In your medical judgement, does Jeffrey Dahmer suffer from a mental disease?'

Answer: 'Had a police officer been standing beside him, he would not have killed. But left to his own resources he lacks control due to his mental disease . . . His disorder is necrophilia, a type of sexual deviation.'

But prosecuting district attorney Micahel McCann insisted that Dahmer was sane and rational, and called Dr Frederick Allan Fosdal, who testified: 'A mental status examination showed Dahmer to be in control, in my professional opinion. He does have a psychiatric disorder, and had this disorder before, during and after his fifteen slayings. This disorder is of a sexual nature, principally necrophilia, but this disorder does not in itself make him lack substantial capacity to conform his behaviour to the requirements of the law.'

The defence called Dahmer's last intended victim, the young black man, Tracy Edwards. He told the jury: 'He seemed friendly and normal at first, but then turned crazy. Like I told the police the first time, "This freak, this crazy guy, is trying to hurt me."'

Defence counsel asked him: 'What impression was made on your mind by the conduct of Jeffrey Dahmer, by the acts of Jeffrey Dahmer, by the manner, experiences and circumstances of Jeffrey Dahmer that you observed?'

Answer: 'It's like I told the police: this guy is crazy.'

Dahmer sat in court wearing a bright orange prison suit. He did not wear his steel-rimmed spectacles because he did not want to look at the witnesses, and he did not look at the young man who had escaped his clutches and brought about his downfall.

Tracy Edwards told the court about his ordeal at the hands of Dahmer. He had gone back to Dahmer's apartment for a drink, but suspected that his rum and coke had been drugged, since he started feeling dizzy. Then Dahmer shoved a twelve-inch butcher's knife into his armpit, the blade directed at his heart.

'If you don't do what I say, I'm going to kill you,' Dahmer said. 'I've done this before. Don't make a move . . . ' Dahmer then handcuffed Edwards's left wrist and led him into the bedroom.

Edwards was waiting for the right moment to escape and was attempting to placate Dahmer. Inside the bedroom he saw that the walls were covered with photographs of nude men in almost every homosexual sex-act imaginable. As he was led to the single bed, Edward noticed to his horror a large bloodstain on the top coverlet, and a human hand protruding from under the bed.

'You'll never leave here,' Dahmer told him. 'It won't be long. I'll show you things you won't believe.' After telling Edwards he planned to eat him, Dahmer put a video cassette of the film The Exorcist on TV and said: 'That was the best movie ever made.' He then went over to a filing cabinet and took out a human skull, saying to Edwards: 'This is how I get people to stay with me – you will stay with me too!' He also showed Edwards photographs of corpses in various stages of dismemberment.

Dahmer forced Edwards to lie on the floor, then put his head to his chest and said: 'I can hear your heart beating. Soon it will be mine. I'm going to cut your heart out.'

Edwards kept chattering to keep Dahmer's mind off killing, and persuaded Dahmer to take him back into the living room for more drinks, although he nearly fainted when he saw the severed human head in the fridge from which Dahmer took the cans of beer. As they sat on the settee, Dahmer began rocking backwards and forwards, sending himself into a drink-induced trance.

'It's time. It's time,' he kept chanting. Edwards knew that if he did not escape now, he never would. Standing up, he punched Dahmer with all his force, then kicked him in the chest, before fleeing the apartment and flagging down two police officers.

Mr Boyle, defence counsel, used blackboard diagrams to chart Dahmer's increasing madness for the jury. 'He begins by living for the weekends, and ends by eating his victims and spending most of his days in bed . . . As a total human being, this is what I see in Jeffrey Dahmer. A person who is into cannibalism, a druggy, sexual fantasies and perversions, rocking and chanting . . . this is Jeffrey Dahmer . . . He started to experiment more and more, because his sickness is growing greater and greater. He began taking pictures of his victims' corpses. He didn't even know that he was mentally ill – he just thought he was *bad*.'

Mr Boyle pointed out that Dahmer had never tried to blame anyone else for his acts, but took the total blame. 'All I wanted was my own selfish gratification . . . ' Boyle pointed a finger at his own head and said bluntly: 'He was *nuts*.' Saying that Dahmer had been unable to conform, he went on: 'This was a crazy man who couldn't stop until he was stopped . . . I submit to you that Jeffrey Dahmer is so out of control that he cannot be punished by ordering imprisonment. He is *out of control*.'

The prosecutor argued that Dahmer had a disordered mind, not a diseased one, and was responsible for his actions. He likened him to an alcoholic: out of control, but with the ability to stop drinking. The testimony of the detective who arrested Dahmer supported this view: 'I began questioning him about the way in which he selected and approached his victims. He stated that before going out for the evening, he generally knew whether or not he planned to commit a homicide . . . He would study the gays in the bar and select one which he found attractive . . . '

Saying that Dahmer's killings had been 'cold-blooded and *planned*,' the prosecutor asked the jury to identify with the victims and not the defendant. He held up photographs of the victims, fanning them out for the jury to see each young face.

On Saturday, 15 February, the jury returned after deliberating for six hours with a 10–2 majority verdict. Squeals of delight greeted the fifteen verdicts – one on each count. Fifteen times Judge Gram asked the jury: 'Did Jeffrey have a mental disease?' Fifteen times the jury said no.

It was incredible that the spectators cheered not because Dahmer had been found guilty, but because he had been found *sane*. In an unusual move, the judge now allowed the relatives of the victims to address the court to tell of their feelings. Most wept, some raged, one girl yelling at Dahmer: 'I hate you, mother-fucker!'

Sentencing was set for the Monday, 17 February, when Dahmer was allowed to address the court. He put on his spectacles for the first time and rose to his feet, the TV cameras zooming in on his face. He said: 'Your honour, you know it is all over now. It has never been a case of trying to get free. I never wanted freedom. Frankly, I wanted death for myself. This has been a case to tell the world that I did what I did not for reasons of hate. I hated no one. I knew I was sick or evil or both. Now I believe I was sick. The doctors told me about my sickness and now I have some peace.

'I realize how much harm I have caused. I did my best to make amends after my arrest, but no matter what I did I could not undo the terrible harm I have caused. My attempts to help identify the remains was the best that I could do, and that was hardly anything.

'I feel so bad for what I did to those poor families,

and I understand their rightful hate. I also know I will be in prison for the rest of my life, and know I will have to turn to God to get me through each day. I should have stayed with God. I tried and failed and created a holocaust. Thank God there will be no more harm that I can do. I believe that only the Lord Jesus Christ can save me from my sins.

'I decided to go through with this trial for a number of reasons. One of these was to let the world know that these were not crimes of hate. I wanted the people of Milwaukee, which I deeply hurt, to know the truth of what I did. I did not want the world to think these were hate-crimes. I did not want any unanswered questions. Now all the questions have been answered . . . '

Dahmer continued: 'I wanted to find out just what it was that caused me to be so bad and evil, but most of all Mr Boyle and I decided that maybe there was a way to tell the world that they could get some help before they end up being hurt or hurting someone. I think the trial did that. And I take the blame for what I did. In closing, I just want to say that I hope God has forgiven me for what I have done. Thank you, your honour, now I am prepared for your sentence, which I know will be the maximum. I ask for no consideration.'

Judge Gram then sentenced Dahmer to fifteen consecutive life terms – totalling 1,070 years – thereby making parole impossible. Dahmer was led away to start serving his sentence in an isolation cell at the Columbia Correctional Institution in Wisconsin, while plans are under way to bring charges against him in Ohio, where he killed his first victim. He identified this victim for the police from a photograph, as Steven Hicks, nineteen, whom he murdered on 18 June 1978.

Dahmer may yet get his wish for death. Ohio has the death penalty on its statute book, and an electric chair waiting . . .

12
THE RUSSIAN CANNIBALS

Officially, the Soviet Union always refused to recognize the existence of crime within its borders. Crime was a product of the corrupt capitalist system and had no place in the 'workers' paradise'. However, with the collapse of the Soviet Union and the dismantling of the totalitarian system which had existed for over seventy years, there has been far greater openness on the part of Russia about events within its borders.

Crime is as much a problem in Russian society as in any other, with the existence of Mafia-type gangs in the larger cities, prostitutes, corrupt officials – and serial killers of the type experienced in Western societies. Even a cannibal to rival Jeffrey Dahmer . . .

The Moscow newspaper *Rossiikaya Gazeta* announced in its April 1992 issue that Russia's bloodiest-ever serial killer would shortly go on trial in Rostov-on-Don in southern Russia, five hundred miles west of Moscow. It was in Rostov that he was arrested in 1990 and where he had committed most of his crimes. The corpses of his victims, blinded and terribly mutilated, were found in forest strips beside railway lines in Russia, Ukraine and Uzbekistan, leading police to dub the wanted man the 'Forest Strip Killer', although the Press called him the 'Rostov Ripper'.

'His twelve years of slaughter struck terror into the hearts of the people not only of the Rostov region, but many other regions as well,' the paper reported.

The police who hunted and tracked down the killer

had operated for many years under the yoke of the old Soviet system, in which warnings that a killer was on the loose could not be freely reported for fear of it being regarded as anti-Soviet propaganda.

As a result, many of his killings were wrongly attributed. When mutilated bodies were found in the woods, the horrific injuries convinced some that it was the work of a weird satanic sect. Others favoured the idea of a gang of mentally retarded child molesters, or even suspected a gang was collecting organs for transplants.

The series of murders began in 1978, when the body of a girl was found in the woods near Rostov. A child molester was finally arrested and executed for this killing, but when more killings of the same type continued, the police realized they had convicted the wrong man.

On 14 April 1992 Andrei Romanovich Chikatilo stood trial inside a cage in the Rostov courtroom, to prevent the relatives of his victims from lynching him. Chikatilo had confessed to the killing of fifty-three girls, women and boys over a twelve-year period.

The case was set to make medical and legal history, simply because Chikatilo had admitted raping his victims, mutilating the bodies and even disembowelling them on occasion, and eating parts of the bodies. Chikatilo had cooperated with the police to the extent of leading them to the sites of many more murders than he was originally suspected of having committed. On his own admission, he was Russia's most prolific serial killer and mass murderer of all time.

When he was led into his steel case inside the courtroom, many of the spectators – relatives of his victims – began wailing in anguish and shouting abuse at him, baying for his blood. Some elderly women beat their breasts and stamped their feet in grief, raging at the man in the cage and demanding that he should be handed over to them as a human sacrifice to satisfy the desire for revenge. The trial had to be delayed for thirty minutes while first-aid workers revived spectators who had fainted.

The judge tried to calm down the screams of rage which had greeted the appearance of Chikatilo, but one plump middle-aged woman shouted: 'We won't calm down. How can we calm down?' Her own young son had been one of the fifty-three victims raped and mutilated by Chikatilo.

The judge told the angry crowd: 'I understand your feelings, but we must have due process of law.' In a previous interview he had told newsmen: 'This case is the only one of its kind in the whole world. There has never been anything like this anywhere.'

He revealed that Chikatilo, a graduate of Rostov University, was arrested twice during the twelve-year investigation but was released through lack of evidence. Fifty investigators and five hundred policemen had worked on the case, with female officers posing as drifters in an attempt to lure the killer to attack. Although the police described Chikatilo's arrest as a 'triumph', one lead writer in a local newspaper retorted: 'It is not such a triumph to have caught a criminal after leaving him on the loose for twelve years.'

As the gangly, gaunt and shaven-headed Chikatilo was escorted into his metal cage, an elderly woman sobbed hysterically: 'You are a damned soul – an evil sadist! How could this be allowed?' Chikatilo merely grinned at her. Two sobbing women tried to break through the police cordon to attack Chikatilo in his cage, but he suddenly tired of the mob, became lost in his own thoughts, removed his grey jacket and stared fixedly at the floor.

Chikatilo appeared oblivious to the mob, grinning crazily, rolling his eyes and reportedly waving pornographic magazines in the air, looking more like an inmate of a mental asylum than one of the world's most ferocious killers. Yet fifty-six-year-old Chikatilo was a well-spoken and educated man, a former schoolteacher described by his friends as a 'kindly, retiring and respected grandfather.' It was hard for the court to reconcile this version of the accused with the monster who confessed to killing twenty-one boys and thirty-two girls and young women during his twelve-year murder spree.

The former literature teacher was charged with killing and sexually mutilating his victims between 1978 and November 1990 when he was arrested. The police had resorted to having a psychological profile of the unknown killer drawn up, using technology and expertise common in the West, but even they were surprised when the killer turned out to be an outwardly gentle teacher.

In his confession, Chikatilo told how he lured his victims to their death by offers of a meal, chewing gum, or even the chance to watch a video at his home. Most of his victims had been young drifters, whom Chikatilo met during his frequent walks to the forest. Telling of his irresistible lust to kill, he said: 'As soon as I saw a lonely person, I would have to drag them off to the woods. I paid no attention to age or sex. I would walk for a couple of hours or so through the woods, and then I would be possessed by a terrible shaking sensation.' Startled officcers had to write down his every word. Never had Chikatilo had such attentive students.

His victims, tied up, then usually knifed to death with a single thrust between the eyes – although some were strangled with a rope, and others had their windpipes bitten through – were later cut up and cannibalized. The gruesome details of the crimes were too much for Chikatilo's wife and two adult children, who changed their names and fled the area following his arrest, fearing reprisals from the relatives of his victims.

Psychiatrist Alexander Bukhanovsky, who examined Chikatilo in custody, and who had drawn up an extremely accurate psychological profile for the police in which he described the suspect as a sexually impotent teacher who seemed respectable and dull to his neighbours, told the court that the accused appeared to be 'the perfect family man – pleasant, quiet, neat and tidy.' However, he went on, Chikatilo had suffered sexual problems since childhood. The confusing social and sexual problems besetting the newly-liberated Russia could soon spawn a similar offender, the doctor warned.

The psychiatrist explained that Chikatilo had inhabited a fantasy world since childhood, and by the time he reached forty he was so deeply immersed in it that the only way he could achieve sexual satisfaction was through the cannibalistic atrocities which have shocked his nation – and the world.

'In his fantasies he was always the conquering hero,' the doctor explained. 'Along with his inferiority complex he also developed delusions of grandeur. Chikatilo decided early on that the world was against him. His psychological problems seem to have begun with the arrest of his father during the Stalinist years. He had committed no crime – it was a political persecution – but this did not prevent the young Chikatilo being bullied and jeered at by his peers.'

Chikatilo grew up in the town of Novocherkassk, some twenty-five miles north-east of Rostov, in an area steeped in the macho culture of the Don Cossacks. By the time he reached puberty, females loomed large in Chikatilo's fantasy life. He wanted them to be meek and submissive. The reality was far different. He found difficulty in establishing relations with girls, who tended to laugh at his clumsy attempts to woo them, and came to blame them for his own impotence.

It was to compensate for his lack of sexual prowess that Chikatilo, a bright young man, turned to the task of self-improvement through education, graduating from Rostov University with a good degree in Russian literature. Even during his compulsory army service he studied at the Lenin Library while his comrades were out chasing girls. Despite the treatment of his father, Chikatilo became a committed Communist.

In 1966 he married a good and gentle woman who

massaged his ego. He was aged twenty-eight at the time. Two years later she gave birth to their daughter, followed a year later by a son. By now Chikatilo was chairman of the regional sports committee, and enjoyed the perks of his position – a second-floor flat in a shabby block. All should have been well with Chikatilo's world.

In the mid-Seventies he moved to a new job, teaching literature in a boarding school in nearby Novo Shatinsk. There he saw the early sexual encounters between boys and girls – encounters he had missed or failed at in his own youth. He grew frustrated and embittered, mad with jealousy and rage. It was not long after that that children began to go missing in Rostov-on-Don, and the twelve-year nightmare had begun.

Bukhanovsky continues to treat Chikatilo in jail, taking the killer his breakfast every morning and chatting to him in the hope of learning more about his strange psychology. He says that Chikatilo constantly refers to a brother, whom he claims was eaten by starving peasants during a famine in the 1930s. The doctor also says that Chikatilo is far more intelligent than he lets on, commenting: 'He was a great theatre-goer. He could sit in a performance of something by Chekhov and be moved to tears, but then go out and murder someone.

'He is also very interested in the American presidents; he can reel off the names, dates and biographies of every one of them.' Referring to the possible execution of Chikatilo, the doctor expresses the hope that even in death, he may be of benefit to science. 'Chikatilo's brain will be of great scientific interest,' Bukhanovsky said. 'It is the sort of opportunity a scientist cannot let pass.'

The trial is expected to last several months, hear sixty witnesses and listen to two hundred and twenty-two volumes of evidence, despite Chikatilo's plea of guilty. Chikatilo had demanded time to read *all* the volumes, but the trial chairman, Leonid Akubzhanov, ruled that he had had plenty of time to do so. Under Russian law, Chikatilo is being tried by a professional judge – Akubzhanov – and two non-professional people's representatives. There was no jury in the courtroom, simply lawyers for the prosecution and defence, and their clerks. If convicted, Chikatilo faces the death penalty, still widely used in the new Commonwealth of Independent States. That penalty is carried out by a firing-squad. In 1991, the Russians executed fifty-nine people in this manner, compared with seventy-six the previous year.

The arrest and trial of Chikatilo marked the end of a twelve-year murder hunt during which twenty-five thousand suspects had been questioned, and one of them, a convicted rapist, was wrongly executed for some of Chikatilo's crimes, is expected to be posthumously pardoned. Another suspect, who committed suicide while awaiting trial for some of Chikatilo's crimes, will also be officially cleared of blame.

The court heard that Chikatilo was first apprehended near the scene of one of his murders in 1979, but managed to convince the police that he was an innocent nature-lover. Five years later he was picked up again, this time with a knife in his attaché case, but managed to talk his way out of being arrested by again claiming that he was out in the woods studying nature.

In the summer of 1984 he spent three months in prison for 'the theft of government property' – three rolls of linoleum. He was also expelled from the party, which meant the loss of privileges. This had the effect of further confirming his belief that the world was against him – even his beloved party. After he was released, and as if in revenge for his incarceration, he killed eight people in a single month.

The butchery was so appalling that top investigators were sent from Moscow to help in the hunt. They confessed that they had never seen anything like it. The killer apparently first cut off his victims' tongues to prevent them from crying out, before bursting their eardrums and gouging out their eyes. While they were still alive he would finally achieve sexual gratification (proved by the presence of semen on the victims' bodies) by carrying out bizarre 'operations'. The boys had their testicles removed, the girls their wombs.

As the death toll mounted, the people of Rostov panicked, with rumours that the killer was a doctor or a homosexual. Children in every school in the region were given questionnaires: have you been approached by any strange man? Have any of your friends reported such a contact? The scope of the investigation was so wide that during its course the police solved 1,062 unrelated crimes, including ninety-five murders.

Originally Chikatilo had sought his victims in the lonely forest strips, but in 1989 he got himself a good job as head of supplies at Rostov's Lenin locomotive repair plant. This job gave him the perfect excuse for hanging around the trains and station, looking for his young prey, picking them up in railway carriages or even on buses. A man of great natural charm, none of his victims gave any indication of having struggled.

'Not one of the victims appears to have shown any sign that they went unwillingly to the woods with him, despite the fact that everyone in Rostov knew there was a cannibal on the loose who always took his prey into the woods,' said chief prosecutor Vitaly Kalyukhin.

Talking about Chikatilo's *modus operandi*, Kalyukhin said that it was always the same: he would approach individuals, often children on their way home from school, and start talking to them. 'He made contact with people very easily,' the prosecutor said. 'I would say he had an amazing talent for it. He could join a bus queue and say to the person in front, "Hey, where did you buy those beautiful mushrooms," and before you knew it he would have the whole crowd chatting.'

With some vague promise he would persuade his intended victim to walk with him into the woods – and then take out the knife which he used to butcher fifty-three people.

Chikatilo's arrest came about as a result of Dr Bukhanovsky's psychological profile, drawn up using techniques pioneered by the FBI. The resulting profile of a retiring, middle-aged, sexually inadequate man suffering from an inferiority complex fitted Chikatilo like a glove, and frustrated officers fell on him with relief.

Chikatilo was finally caught seven days after burying his last victim. On 6 November he was stopped for a routine check by a policeman, who noticed a drop of blood on his cheek. When a body was found a few days later, Chikatilo was placed under surveillance. Vitaly Kalyukhin said: 'By that time we knew that he picked up victims in suburban trains, and we had people in every wagon of every suburban train out of Rostov.'

On 20 November, police officers watched Chikatilo approach two boys, both of whom backed away. The decision was made to arrest Chikatilo immediately. He was far too dangerous to be allowed to run free any longer, in the hope of catching him in the act. The suspect was taken to police headquarters, where after very little persuasion and questioning, Chikatilo unburdened himself of his crimes, even to the extent of taking officers to sites in the forest where he had hidden other bodies – bodies of people not known to be dead, but simply names on the missing persons' register.

Although the city of Rostov is a mafia centre known to Russians as the 'father of crime' – (Odessa is the 'mother') – the police had never believed that the killer belonged to the criminal underworld of the city, but suspected rather that, like so many other serial killers, he would be an apparently respectable citizen. But even they were shocked by their catch. Chikatilo, a Ukrainian living in the nearby town of Novocherkassk, turned out to be a languages graduate, a former teacher, and one-time member of the Communist Party. He was married, with children of his own and even grandchildren. It seemed unthinkable . . . The judge had begun the trial proceedings by saying: 'There will be no secrets. Let us all try to learn at least something from these proceedings.'

The reading of the charges then began, a process which took several days, and it was soon evident from the ages and occupations of the victims that most had been drifters, with no families to miss them. They were either smothered or stabbed, their bodies being savagely mutilated about the genital areas. Some had their eyes gouged out, while others had been disembowelled.

According to *Izvestia*, it was not until the death toll had reached twenty that the police realized that they were dealing with a 'super-killer'. During the long years of the hunt for him, hidden cameras had photographed thousands of men walking with teenagers, and policemen acted as decoys in trains and other public places. Over 163,000 men had been forced to give blood samples. (The police had for years been seeking a man with a specific blood group, detected from his semen left in the bodies of his victims. Not until 1990 did scientists discover that one man in a million has sperm and blood groups which don't match. Chikatilo is that one man in a million. It was his unique body make-up which had allowed him to go free for so long.) The killer remained at large, seemingly invisible. *Tass* news agency revealed that at least one innocent man had been executed for some of Chikatilo's crimes.

The trial of Chikatilo continued, with the killer himself telling the court about his life and crimes. He complained that he was a victim of a totalitarian system, having been a graduate of the Marxist-Leninist Institute. The *Tass* news agency reported that Chikatilo told the court: 'I am a freak of nature, a mad beast, a mistake of nature.'

Testifying for the first time from inside his steel cage, Chikatilo told of his poor life, of constant business trips where he was forced to stay at dirty railway stations and miserable hotels. He complained that his bosses were rude to him.

He acknowledged that he was indeed the man the

newspaper had called the 'Rostov Ripper', and admitted killing and mutilating twenty-one boys, fourteen girls and eighteen women since 1978. Fourteen of the females were said to have been aged between nine and seventeen.

Telling of how he had killed his victims with a knife, a rope, or even his teeth, Chikatilo said he was unsure of how many people he had killed. 'Possibly fifty-five, maybe more,' he told the judge in a matter-of-fact tone. Although he raped most of his victims before killing them, he admitted having had sex with at least one corpse.

He told of his joy and satisfaction at eating the sexual organs of his teenage victims, and then spoke once more about his brother, eaten, he claims, by starving peasants, and presumably the source of his fantasy. Unless even the brother is fantasy . . .

One thing is certain: the trial will have many more shocking revelations to come.

In August 1991 Russian police revealed that they were hunting a cannibal, known as 'Metal Fang'. Nikolai Dzhumagaliev was locked away after butchering dozens of women in his home city of Alma-Ata, in Kazakhstan. He used to stalk attractive women and invite them for a stroll along the river. Then he raped his victims, and hacked them to death with knives and axes he carried in his rucksack.

He roasted several bodies in the open air, his speciality being to serve his victims to unsuspecting dinner guests. He was caught when he began inviting women back to the hostel where he lived. Two drunks who stumbled into the kitchen found him in the middle of preparing one of his meals. They found a woman's head and intestines in a basin and called the police.

Now Dzhumagaliev has escaped from a top-security mental hospital, and the women of Moscow are said to be in a state of panic. Moscow police admit that they have no clue as to his whereabouts. A police spokesman said: 'He is well-mannered and speaks without an accent. He is always clean-shaven and neatly dressed. His image is that of a perfect gentleman, though it has to be said that the teeth are a bit odd. He persuaded his dentist to fit them because he reckoned they looked good.' (They are made of stainless steel.) 'We suspect Dzhumagaliev is trying to establish a base in cheap accommodation,' the police added, revealing that the wanted man had been on the run for two years, but only now had they decided to alert the public. 'We have our reasons,' the spokesman said. 'We believe the danger to be far greater than when he first left the hospital.'

13
CONCLUSIONS

It isn't so far away after all, is it? Not some bizarre custom from a remote past, but something happening now, today. It is part of our heritage; something we brought with us from the caves and which lives within us still in our swanky apartments or semi-detached shelters. It is just barely under the skin, the compulsion to eat human flesh.

It only waits for famine, or natural catastrophe, or the madness of the individual living in the heart of an insane city for cannibalism to surface and assume its old place at the table. Thomas de Quincey was stating no more than the obvious when he wrote: 'Gentlemen, I'll tell you the plain truth. Every day of the year we take up a paper, we read the opening of a murder.'

In 1971 a member of the Black September terrorist organization was accused of assassinating Wasfi Tal, the prime minister of Jordan, boasting to his accusers: 'I am satisfied now. I drank from Tal's blood.' Other witnesses corroborated his statement: he was talking literally.

At the height of the Gulf crisis in August 1990, the Iraqi Government issued a statement threatening that if America should attack Iraq with its war-planes, 'If just one American is shot down by our forces, his body will immediately be eaten by the Iraqi people.' This threat to eat American pilots was not mere bravado. And so now we can claim that cannibalism exists in the political and economic spheres too.

Dr Magnus Pyke revealed in *The Times* of 11 March

1973 that during the war, the Minister of Food, Lord Woolton, rejected a suggestion from his scientific advisors that blood donated surplus to transfusion requirements should be used to make black pudding for distribution on ration. Lord Woolton took the view that consuming blood by transfusion was one thing, actually eating it was quite another.

What we have seen in this survey is that there exists no natural aversion to cannibalism. It is not man's oldest taboo – but his oldest diet. Any modern aversion was brought about solely by religion, which regarded a dead body as being sacred. On the day of judgement, or in the next world, we would all need our old bodies to rise again; they were not to be regarded as emergency rations.

In 1728 Jonathan Swift published his *Modest Proposal* . . . He was using irony to lash the consciences of absentee English landlords who evicted starving Irish men and women from their homes when they could no longer pay the rent, forcing them out to die like animals in the wilds. He wrote:

I have been assured by a very knowing American of my acquaintance in London, that a young healthy child well nurs'd is, at a year old, a most delicious, nourishing and wholesome food, whether stewed, roasted, baked or boiled; and I make no doubt that it will equally serve in a fricasée, or a ragoût . . .

His *Modest Proposal* . . . was designed to reduce beggary and thieving by encouraging mothers to raise their children for one year and then sell them to their landlords. 'I grant this food will be somewhat dear, but it will still be perfectly suitable for the landlords . . . who, as they have already devoured most of the parents, seem to have the best title to the children . . . I believe no gentleman would repine to give ten shillings for the carcase of a good fat child.'

But Swift was too good a writer to merely publish his

Proposal as irony. He knew he would be appealing to deep and atavistic instincts in his readers; that his piece would be read by some as a penny-shocker. They would find it titillating, even exciting, causing them to speculate: what *would* a human baby taste like? We have our answer: human flesh when cooked tastes just like pork . . .

What we have not discussed is the *psychological* drive which leads some people to commit cannibalism when there exists no extreme of starvation, no dire necessity. The question of sanity is always raised in cases like that of Jeffrey Dahmer, and indeed most cases of this type do involve elements of sexual or religious sadism and fanaticism; there is often a history of strong paranoid delusion. But the desire to bite exists in us all, and although the step from biting to cannibalism is a great step, the desire is hidden within our subconscious.

Psychoanalysts find it interesting that many forms of assault involve biting, and that even minor forms of hostility are expressed via the mouth, in the form of insults or shouts. Freudians, who coined the term 'oral fixation', postulate that cannibalism is simply a reversion to a primitive infant state where all the infant's needs are satisfied via the mouth, so that aggression is expressed by biting, and pleasure from sucking. True, infants often do express aggression by biting, so that the cannibal sexual sadist may be taking to the extreme the lover's nibble . . .

Other experts feel that the act of cannibalism might be a reversion to primitive impulses, a return or slipping back to our ancestral primeval state when cannibalism was a common activity. But this is a highly contentious area, since not all experts agree that primitive man was a cannibal.

Of course, not all cannibalism is witting.

A newspaper report dated 30 March 1991, under the headline CANNIBAL TAKEAWAY, claims that a restaurant in China was serving dumplings stuffed with human flesh.

Wang Guang offered them in his White Temple restaurant from 1987, according to the newspaper *Hainan Special Zone Daily*. The dumplings were a big hit with customers.

Guang's brother, a crematorium worker, supplied him with flesh hacked from corpses. The newspaper reports: 'He ground them up, mixed the flesh with lots of spices for fear that customers would taste the difference. He billed them as Sichuan-style dumplings.' The western province of Sichuan is famous for its spicy food. 'The dumplings were very popular because they were cheap and delicious,' the report said. 'The restaurant often sold out.'

The brothers were found out when the parents of a young woman killed in a road accident discovered that her body had been mutilated. The newspaper said that the authorities were trying to work out what charges they could bring against the brothers.

Cannibalism is often used as a subject for humour, mostly cartoons of the missionaries in the cooking-pot variety. One version has one missionary saying to the other: 'Cheer up, Carruthers. We'll have the last laugh – I've pissed in their soup.'

The theme of cannibalism has been used in the novel, in Greek mythology and in the cinema. *Soylent Green* (1973) depicted a future world where human bodies are processed in secret hi-tech plants and distributed as food to the populace. In *The Naked Gun* (1989) the severed finger in the hot dog was used for comic effect. *The Night of the Living Dead* is a cult sixties horror movie in which zombies prowl the streets, seeking out the living to eat. The rise of the 'snuff movie' has resulted in acts of cannibalism actually being filmed and distributed for profit.

The Emperor's Naked Army Marches On (1990), is a semi-documentary Japanese film about the obsession of Kenzo Okuzaki, a World War Two soldier, to expose atrocities committed by Japanese troops in New Guinea, twenty-three days before the end of the war, when

Okuzaki's senior officer ordered the execution of twelve soldiers for alleged desertion. In reality, it was to provide meat for his troops. A medical orderly, now working in a restaurant in Kobe, speaks of 'white pork' (Allied soldiers) and 'black pork' (New Guinea natives). The latter was scarce because the locals ran so fast.

Another modern movie, Peter Greenaway's *The Cook, the Thief, His Wife and Her Lover* (1989) is a moody and atmospheric film, highly literate, and with a metaphysical dimension which neatly ties together the themes and connections between eroticism, eating and death, with cannibalism as a revenge motif.

Voltaire (1694–1778) touched briefly on the subject of cannibalism in his novel *Candide*. A far more ambitious attempt to include cannibalism in the modern novel came with the publication of the controversial *American Psycho* by Bret Easton Ellis (Pan 1991). It met with harsh treatment from the critics. Some dismissed it as mere pornography, failing to recognize its true purpose. An unpleasant novel, it had to be written in the same way that De Sade had to be published. It is in fact a very moral novel which exposes the false values and hypocrisies of a certain way of life in Western societies.

Patrick Bateman, the 'psycho' of the title – (conscious echoes of Norman Bates from the original 'Psycho') – is introduced to us by his girlfriend as 'the boy next door'. He is a wealthy young Wall Street broker. But on page twenty he whispers to us: 'No I'm not. I'm a fucking evil psychopath.' He lives in a designer-label milieu and is a typical product of the consumer society. Revealingly, he hates live music – he prefers the sound of compact discs. He prefers pornography to real sex 'because it is less complicated'. He is isolated from reality, not sure whether life is real or television. He warns us that we know only one facet of his personality: Student. But then talks about his rages at Harvard, his sense of disgust, hinting at murders he committed at that time.

The horrific descriptions of actual murders are what

disgusted the critics. Describing the murder of one girl Bateman says he tried to bite off her thumb, 'I managed to gnaw the flesh off, leaving the bone exposed.' And again: 'I stand over Bethany's body, sipping a drink contemplatively, studying its condition. Both eyelids are open halfway and her lower teeth look as if they are jutting out since her lips have been torn – actually bitten – off. Earlier in the day I had sawn off her left arm . . . a lot of it had been hacked or gnawed off.' There are later descriptions of eating human brains.

The moral purpose of the author comes across with the killer's self-description. 'There wasn't a clear, identifiable emotion within me, except for greed and, possibly, total disgust. I had all the characteristics of a human being – flesh, blood, skin, hair – but my depersonalization was so intense, had gone so deep, that the normal ability to feel compassion had been eradicated, the victim of a slow, purposeful erasure. I was simply imitating reality, a rough resemblance of a human being, with only a dim corner of my mind working.'

The survivalist cult is big in the United States. Americans teach themselves to survive a nuclear war, to live in underground bunkers and be totally independent, living entirely on what they can grow or catch. Or, in a pinch, on each other. It is a cruel commentary on human nature that we are all too ready to devour one another.

Leonard Lake was arrested in California in February 1985 after attempting to intercede for his partner Charles Ng on a shoplifting charge: Ng had stolen a vice, and when Lake offered to pay for it, Ng took the opportunity to flee. The arrest triggered off other investigations. At a cabin in Calveras County, home videos were found which depicted Lake and Charles Ng in the act of killing women on screen, after raping them. Police discovered the concrete bunker which the pair had used as a torture chamber and a film studio, and where prisoners had been held. They also found, in shallow graves, the remains of nineteen women and children, some as young as two years of age. Their deaths had been recorded on film, as had the plastic bags containing human bones boiled down into soup.

Leonard Lake's diary detailed his plans to stock concrete bunkers with food and weapons to survive a nuclear war – and to have a cadre of captives held in isolated chambers, for sexual gratification and food. His diary records his plans to build a shelter 'which will provide a facility for my sexual fantasies. It will provide physical security for myself and my passions. It will protect me from nuclear fallout. Tapes, photographs, and weapons will be hidden away.'

Lake was, unsurprisingly, heavily into witchcraft and Satanism, and read medieval legends and the folk-lore of early civilizations as if they might provide an answer to his problems.

He died in a San Francisco hospital after taking a cyanide capsule while in police custody. There was no clue to Lake's identity following his death, but the car he had been driving was traced to a missing car salesman, Paul Cosner. And that in turn led to the cabin in Calveras County . . .

Charles Ng was subsequently arrested in Canada and was sentenced to a four-and-a-half-year prison term for shoplifting. He denied any involvement in the murders, claiming that Lake did them alone.

Lake, a Vietnam veteran, saw himself as a latter-day Viking, a warrior figure who would survive the collapse of society. In reality, he was a psychopath who preyed on other people and devoured them.

We can perhaps understand eating human flesh from necessity, however unpleasant the images which are conjured up. But it is a long way from being adrift in a lifeboat to being adrift in society, and for some people this feeling of alienation brings out the worst in them, and they revert to a primitive level of savagery. Witness Denis Nilsen, who was so miserable and lonely that he killed fifteen young men just to have something to

255

nect' to. He kept the body of one youth in an armchair for a week, saying that it was 'nice to have someone to come home to'.

Cannibalism is a grim subject. But in a civilization which over-populates and destroys the planet, it might even become an environmental issue: eating the dead might be seen as being better than polluting the earth.

To the reader who is tempted to become a vegetarian, I can only sympathize. During the writing of this book I have found myself unable to eat meat. The thought of it makes me feel physically sick. I have been programmed to ignore my primitive past. But I have never in my life been really hungry, nor starved, and I wonder if, in those circumstances, I would be tempted to eat my fellow men . . .

BIBLIOGRAPHY

Angelella, Michael, *Trail of Blood – The Albert Fish Story*, Bobbs-Merrill, New York, 1979.

Bolitho, William, *Murder for Profit*, Dobson, 1926.

Boorstin, Daniel J., *The Discoverers*, Dent, 1984.

Bjerre, Jens, *The Last Cannibals*, Michael Joseph, 1956.

de River, J. Paul, *The Sexual Criminal*, Charles C. Thomas, Illinois, 1949.

Diaz, Bernal, *The Conquest of New Spain*, Harmondsworth, 1963.

Duke, Thomas S., *Celebrated Criminal Cases of America*, James H. Barry, San Francisco, 1910.

Elkin, A. P., *The Australian Aborigines*, Angus & Robertson, 1938.

Englade, Ken, *Cellar of Horror*, St Martin's Press, New York, 1988.

Frazer, Sir James G., *The Golden Bough*, twelve vols, Macmillan, 1890–1915.

Gaute, J. H. H., and Odell, Robin, *The Murderer's Who's Who*, Harrap, 1986.

Green, Jonathon, *The Directory of Infamy*, Mills & Boon, 1980.

Griffiths, Major Arthur, *Mysteries of Police and Crime*, Cassell, 1899.

Gwyther, J., *Captain Cook and the South Pacific*, Houghton-Mifflin, Boston, 1954.

Hogg, Gary, *Cannibalism and Human Sacrifice*, Robert Hale, 1958.

James, E. O., *Origins of Sacrifice*, John Murray, 1933.

Kyle-Little, Syd, *Whispering Wind*, Hutchinson, 1957.

Leakey, L. S. B., *Mau Mau and the Kikuyu*, Methuen, 1952.

Leigh, Ilone, *In the Shadow of the Mau Mau*, W. H. Allen, 1954.

Leyton, Elliot, *Hunting Humans*, Penguin, 1989.

Lunde, Donald T., *Murder and Madness*, W. W. Norton, New York, 1979.

Marriner, Brian, *Forensic Clues to Murder*, Arrow, 1991.

Masters, Brian, *Killing for Company*, Jonathan Cape, 1985.

Nash, Jay Robert, *Murder, America*, Harrap, 1981.

Norris, Joel, *Serial Killers*, Arrow, 1990.

Notable British Trials (A series of 83 titles), James Hodge, Glasgow, c. 1850–

Prest, Thomas Peckett, *The Story of Pearls: The Barber of Fleet Street, A Domestic Romance*, London, 1850.

Read, Piers Paul, *Alive: The Story of the Andes Survivors*, Secker & Warburg, 1974.

Russell of Liverpool, Lord, *The Scourge of the Swastika*, Cassell, 1954.

Sifakis, Carl, *The Encyclopaedia of American Crime*, Facts on File, New York, 1982.

Södermann, H., *Auf der Spur des Verbrechen*, Köln-Berlin, 1924.

St. Johnston, A., *Camping Among Cannibals*, Macmillan, 1883.

Swift, Jonathan, *A Modest Proposal* for Preventing the Children of Ireland from being a Burden to their Parents or Country, Dublin, 1728; London, 1730.

Tannahill, Reay, *Flesh and Blood: A History of the Cannibal Complex*, Hamish Hamilton, 1975.

Wilson, Colin, *A Casebook of Murder*, Leslie Frewin, 1969.

Wilson, Colin, *Order of Assassins: A Psychology of Murder*, Hart-Davis, 1972.

Wilson, Colin, and Pitman, Patricia, *Encyclopaedia of Murder*, Putnam, 1962.

Wilson, Colin, and Seaman, Donald, *Encyclopaedia of Modern Murder*, Arthur Barker, 1983.

Also: *True Detective Magazine*. Grateful thanks for access to their files covering the past thirty-eight years.

INDEX

267

268